Dogfight

CALVIN TRILLIN

Dogfight

The 2012 Presidential Campaign in Verse

RANDOM HOUSE

NEW YORK

Published in the United States by Random House,
an imprint of The Random House Publishing Group, a division
of Random House, Inc., New York.

RANDOM HOUSE and colophon are registered
trademarks of Random House, Inc.

The narrative poem that constitutes the bulk of this book appears
here for the first time. Most of the poems embedded
in it originally appeared in *The Nation*. The prose pieces originally appeared in
The New Yorker, Slate, or *The New York Times.*

ISBN 978-0-8129-9368-4
eBook ISBN 978-0-8129-9369-1

Printed in the United States of America on acid-free paper

www.atrandom.com

2 4 6 8 9 7 5 3

For my old pal Peter Wolf

Contents

1.

2008

The '08 votes for President were in.
They showed Barack Obama with the win—
A solid win, a win that was historic.
Americans were moved to wax euphoric.
Yes, even some who'd voted for McCain
Were proud we'd have a man of color reign
As President. Historians took note.
Amidst the cheers, one versifier wrote,
"And foreigners from Rome to Yokohama
Were cheering an American: Obama.
From this vote, they were willing to infer
We aren't the people they had thought we were.
And Lady Liberty, as people call her,
Was standing in the harbor somewhat taller."
The task this man would face, of course, was humbling:
The whole economy had started crumbling.

As people lost their jobs and houses too,
The experts disagreed on what to do.
Some banks were saved, and some were left to fail.
As Hamlet said, "To bail or not to bail . . ."

The People in Charge

The people in charge of the bailout attempts
Are titans of Wall Street, with fortunes accrued.
They seem a bit clueless about what to do.
Remember when they were the guys who seemed shrewd?

Yes, Washington says, from both sides of the aisle,
That these are the shoulders upon which to lean.
But we'd feel more confident if we were sure
That they knew what "credit default swap" might mean.

And Congress seemed to any average voter
Irreparable, much like a seized-up motor.
One hope persisted once Obama'd won:
That he would change the way that things were done.
His victory, some said, could also mean
The GOP was fading from the scene—
A party that was clearly in its throes.
The Sabbath Gasbags on the Sunday shows
Said at the least from now on we would see

A dismal decade for the GOP—
A period filled with sadness and regrets,
With losses like the early sixties Mets.
The Gasbags, though, had said the same before—
To be precise, in 1964.
They'd said the landslide won by LBJ
Might cause the GOP to fade away.
But this was all forgotten by the date
Of Nixon's win in 1968.
The Gasbags have a minor brain affliction:
They can't remember any wrong prediction.

The State of the Union, 2009

The State of the Union's the President's chance to speak,
   perorate, and evoke.
For this year's an honest first sentence would be "The State
   of the Union is broke."

To counter what Obama would orate
To Congress on the nation's shaky state,
The top Republicans chose Bobby Jindal,
In hopes a rising star like him could kindle
Some sort of spark conservatives would find
Inspiring, and not become resigned
To wandering in the wilderness once more

While Democratic liberals ran the store.
But Jindal, thought to be a true past master
Of speaking, was, in fact, a true disaster.
This governor's ideas seemed rather skimpy.
The governor himself seemed rather wimpy.
He proved to be an easy man to mock:
He's like the dorky page on *30 Rock*.

Bad Opening Night for the G.O.P.

Yes, poor Bobby Jindal has flubbed his premiere.
If this is the guy who they think is a star,
There's one thing to say, and to say loud and clear:
Come back, Sarah Palin, wherever you are.

In stories from the capital we read
That now the GOP was close to dead
And Democrats would soon be dancing jigs,
Their opposition fading out like Whigs.

2.

←——————→

2010

Recovery moved slowly, step by step—
Called sluggish, though most slugs have much more pep.
Obama's health-care bill was passed—a feat
Republicans then demonized *tout suite,*
Although its main ideas all began
As part of a Republican-backed plan.
(The White House seemed afflicted with some shyness
While letting them brand quite a plus a minus.)
Some critics said that health care could have waited
Until our unemployment woes abated.
Barack Obama's promised hope and change
Seemed far away and maybe out of range.
The Sabbath Gasbags then began to say
Obama's mojo may have drained away.

Pundits Say Washington Must Instill Confidence

The pundits say Obama must discuss
Our plight but sound much less like Gloomy Gus:
We need the-only-thing-we-have-to-fear leaders,
Or, failing that, the Dallas Cowboy cheerleaders.

And meanwhile all across this wounded land
Some angry people said they'd take their stand.
They said that what the Framers had in mind
Was not a government that seemed inclined
To dominate our lives at work and play
And grow much more intrusive every day.
They said that those who'd worked, obeyed the rules,
Were now supporting layabouts and fools.
These folks were quick to vocally condemn
All handouts (but the ones that went to them).
Quite quickly, they were ready to proclaim
They were a movement, and they took a name
From Boston patriots who took such glee
In tossing British tea into the sea.

Tea Party
(With particularly abject apologies to the creators of
*   "Matchmaker" from Fiddler on the Roof)*

Tea Party! Tea Party! We're mad as hell.
Government's huge, and growing pell-mell.
Immigrant numbers continue to swell.
No wonder we're all mad as hell.

Tea Party! Tea Party! We hate those hacks
Governing now. They love to tax.
We're mad as hell and we'll never relax
'Til government gets off our backs.

We're sick of supporting those slackers
Who think everything's free.
Though we have billionaire backers,
We talk just as populist as can be.

Tea Party! Tea Party! We would dispel
Notions that we're too bourgeois to rebel.
We'll start electing some new personnel,
'Cause, trust us: we're all mad as hell.

In midterms what these rebels meant to do
Was bid their party's moderates adieu.
Their candidates in that election season

Were those who think that compromise is treason.
Sure, some of them ran weird campaigns wherein
They showed themselves just too bizarre to win.

Late Night Comics Bid Farewell to Christine O'Donnell, Tea Party Senatorial Candidate from Delaware

You surely were a hoot, Christine.
We're sad to see you leave the scene.
We reveled in the revelation
That you'd condemned all masturbation.
(Not only us but even anchors
Enjoyed the way you fought those wankers.)
Until you came along one day,
Old witchcraft jokes had been passé.
Because of you, just for a while,
Those witchcraft jokes were back in style.
So though, Christine, we now say ciao,
We hope you're back two years from now.

But many got elected, and were sent
To Washington, the place they most resent.
The House, now with a GOP majority,
Could face Barack Obama with authority.
The legislative battle recommenced:

Whatever he was for they were against.
Their heritage from Reagan now would show:
Not Ronald—Nancy, preaching "Just say no."

On Revelations of Where the Secret Funding for the Tea Party Comes From

They're meant to be a grassroots gang
Of populists who quickly sprang
From nowhere 'cause they've had enough
Of liberal bureaucratic guff.
Less government is what they're for—
The very goal pushed heretofore
By every oil man who's a foe
Of regs that slow up making dough.
And guess who's funding them? No joke:
Two wealthy oilmen name of Koch,
With faux foundations in cahoots,
Provide the funds. Some grass! Some roots!

The weak economy proved hard to heal.
At times, the president seemed too genteel—
Unwilling still to knock some heads the way
Some heads were knocked around by LBJ.
His speeches far surpassed the other guys'.
His gamble caused Bin Laden's quick demise.

But still the polls showed many folks believed
His promises, so far, were unachieved.
The punditry, its '08 views forgotten,
Now said his reelection odds were rotten.

3.

Mentionables

Since order is for them a big concern,
Republicans will often go in turn.
Whatever fight is fought, they still incline
To nominate the guy who's next in line—
Like Dole, for instance, or like John McCain,
Some stalwart who had run before in vain.
It's moving up in turn that usually does it.
In this round, though, whose turn, exactly, was it?
Was it, perchance, between those who'd begun
The nomination race McCain had won?
Of Huckabee and Romney from that tussle,
The former could command some right-wing muscle.
But would he run? He'd hinted that he might,
Then said he had no stomach for the fight.
(Although the actual stomach he'd once shed
Was starting once again to get widespread.)

With books and speeches, plus his Fox News show,
Mike seemed inclined to make some serious dough.

Politico Reveals That All Non-Office-Holding Contenders for the Republican Presidential Nomination in 2012 Except Mitt Romney Are on the Fox News Payroll

Of hopefuls with viewpoints that fit,
Now Murdoch employs all but Mitt.
And Tea Party folks can't go broke,
Since things do go better with Koch.
Yes, that's the crusade that competes
To rid simple folks of elites.

Another candidate one might define
As qualifying as the next in line
Was Sarah Palin—yes, an '08 vet
Who hinted she might throw her hat in yet,
Although her '08 run for veep had flopped.
(A long Hail Mary pass that Palin dropped.)
Some elements within the party brass
Were hoping she'd decide to take a pass.
One hint she might: both Palin and her kin
Seemed concentrating hard on cashing in
Through any TV show that they could wangle—

Kardashians, but with a North Woods angle.
So even when her act went on the road,
She wasn't clearly back in campaign mode.

The Pundits Analyze Sarah Palin's Bus Tour

Now Palin's seen out on the stump.
But is she just a female Trump—
A person eager for each mention
For purposes of brand extension?

So—disappointing fans, who'd been devout—
She seemed inclined to sit this campaign out.
So whose turn now? Though Romney was on deck,
Conservatives thought they had better check
Around for someone less like Mister Cleaver
And more like them—that is, a true believer.
Barack Obama's numbers still were low,
Which meant that lots of folks might have a go
At capturing the chance to lead a fight
That seemed to have sweet victory in sight.
Pawlenty brought advisers to his state.
In Mississippi, Barbour lost some weight.
(Still, relative to others on the list, he
Remained quite fat, though not as fat as Christie.)
And Bachmann, still the faithfuls' faithful fighter,

Emerged as Palin lite—or even liter.
And so the mentioners all mentioned those
Whom President Obama might oppose.
But two of those who often got a mention
Said running this time wasn't their intention.
Yes, Haley Barbour, and Mitch Daniels, too,
Announced before they started they were through.

Mitch Daniels Announces That He Will Not Run for President

We bid Mitch Daniels fond adieu
And say, "Mitch, we admire you
For saying that what you love best
Is family, and not this quest."
Most candidates, without a doubt,
Seem best to us when they drop out.

Though thoughts of Bushes didn't bring a glow,
Jeb Bush was asked, and he said, "Thank you, no."
So, next in line? Well, only Romney, who
Was unloved by the right-wing tried and true.
This caused the pundits to restate this view:
Without a queue, a scramble might ensue.

4.

Trump Trumped

One Donald Trump seeks sustenance in fame—
Much like a bloated moth that's drawn to flame.
Election season! Up pops Donald Trump.
Gas-filled as if by some gigantic pump,
He reappears—a loud performance artist
At boasting he's the richest and the smartest.
So rich and smart, quadrennially he'll drone,
That he deserves the White House—or a throne.
Then, once he's had his say . . . and say . . . and say,
He, blessedly, will finally go away.
But this time on the tube he seemed to bray
That he had chips and he had come to play.
To hear him say he'd wade into the fray
Made all the party leaders say *"Oy vey,"*
Because at one point, several polls agreed,
Among Republicans he held the lead.

The ace Trump said had made his winning hand?
Obama's birth was in some other land,
And so he was illegal in his slot,
Since natural born he certainly was not.
The Donald said he knew from private eyes
That Democrats were in for a surprise.

Donald Trump, Expressing Interest in Running for President Himself, Says He Wants to See President Obama's Birth Certificate

All White House hopefuls we forewarn:
You'll have to prove that you were born.
Before Trump hits the state of granite,
He must identify the planet
Where he first took on human form—
A place where blowhards are the norm.

But then the White House posted on its site
The document that "birthers" on the right
Had said did not exist. And so the proof
That Trump had promised vanished with a poof!
He blathered on, to keep the spotlight's glare.
The talk about him switched then to his hair.

New York Insiders Offer Another Interpretation of How Committed Trump Was to a Presidential Campaign

The real estate sharks say that Trump would have left
Once serious financial disclosure awaited,
Because that disclosure would prove to the world
His boasts of his riches are greatly inflated.

But Donald Trump had led, and that revealed
A lot about the stature of the field.
Though first-tier candidates were mostly out,
Republicans were asking, "What about
The second tier, or what about the third?
Has nothing from those other tiers been heard?
As chances in the fall improve a lot,
Could this bunch really be the best we've got?"
Discussions of the race were not who'd win it
But who else might agree to getting in it.

Late Night Comics Respond to Trump's Exit

They've snatched the note from Donald's one-note tune.
Our pet buffoon has left the room so soon!

To make our jokes at night we always gotta
Find someone who can serve as our piñata.
That won't be hard to find in this campaign.
Right now we've got our eyes on Herman Cain.

5.

←——————→

First One Out

A budget that Paul Ryan thought astute
Was praised by other candidates. But Newt
Not only failed to join in all the cheering
But called it right-wing social engineering.
Instead of going to county fairs to schmooze,
The Gingriches enjoyed a Grecian cruise.
At Tiffany's, we learned, Newt had in force
A credit line whose size could choke a horse.
Newt's staff all quit. They said he was a pain.
But Newt himself announced he would remain.
Reporters, who'd thought he'd be first to leave,
Were wondering what Newt had up his sleeve.
Among the candidates, the first "I'm out"
Was heard from Tim Pawlenty, who, no doubt,
Was seen by pundits some weeks in advance
As having more than just a passing chance

To win a straw poll that is held in Ames—
The winner of which generally claims
To be the candidate who's first to show
He could be in possession of Big Mo.

The Ames Straw Poll

Although the poll is hardly scientific,
Results are studied like a hieroglyphic.
They're analyzed at length for what they show,
As if they were the entrails of a crow.

Pawlenty, as a man from one state north,
Had pinned his hopes on being thus thrust forth.
It's true he'd shown some weakness in debate,
But Iowa, some thought, could be Tim's state.
Right-wing, and evangelical to boot,
He had a quality that seemed to suit
The Hawkeye voters: When he's at his best,
Pawlenty's manner clearly shouts, "Midwest!"
And as for right-wing dogma, he could sell it
Without impressing voters as a zealot.
There were, in fact, among the cognoscenti
Some folks who'd placed their bets on Tim Pawlenty.
They thought that Tim might be the man to beat
Mitt Romney (who at Ames did not compete).

Tim's hopes for being lead beast in the herd
Were dashed in Ames: Pawlenty came in third —
Far back in third. It wasn't even close.
So, quickly, Tim Pawlenty said *adios*.
Too quickly, several pundits would propound.
Pawlenty, they advised, should stick around.
But Tim Pawlenty wasn't looking back.
So thus ordained as leader of the pack
Was Congresswoman Bachmann, who'd gained ground
All summer, 'til in August she was crowned
The straw poll winner, meaning, so to speak,
She got discussed as flavor of the week.
And nationally she started to emerge
While overtaking Romney in a surge.
No longer was it fair to introduce
Michele as "Sarah Palin minus moose."

Michele: A Serenade by Iowa Social Conservatives

(With apologies to the Beatles)

Michele, our belle,
Thinks that gays will all be sent to hell.
That's Michele.

Michele, our belle,
Thinks they're sick but could be made all well.
Yes, Michele.

She just needs to turn them toward Jesus.
They're going through a phase
That leads to filthy ways.
But with her hubby's help these guys could
All be John Wayne.

Michele, our belle,
Views you have are suiting us just swell.
Our Michele.

6.

←———→

A Brief Reign on Top

The next "I'm out" upset Michele's domain:
Ed Rollins, who had managed her campaign,
Announced that he would leave—a key defection.
Her quest since Ames had somehow lost direction.
The scrutiny front-runners always get
Exposed some things the Bachmanns might regret.
Their clinic was a source of great debate,
Since it seemed keen on turning gay men straight.

Unintended Consequences for Marcus Bachmann

The Bachmanns' belief that gay men should be straight
Caused all sorts of jokes, innuendo and such.
The bloggers and late-night comedians pounced:
They said maybe Marcus protested too much.

Some rumors that were passed around in stealth
Implied Michele was not in perfect health.
As indicated by the groans and laughs,
Ms. Bachmann could be counted on for gaffes.
Before she ran, she'd casually been able
To shade or to exaggerate on cable.
Now, things she said—some wrong, some just inscrutable—
Were not, in this campaign, considered suitable:
The history was flawed, the science too.
(She said, although it's not remotely true,
That shots now given girls across the nation
Have been the cause of mental retardation.)
When northeast states were walloped by Irene,
She said God's wrath had surely set that scene.

So Why Be So Hard on Vermont?

*Michele Bachmann says Hurricane Irene was God's
warning to curb excessive government spending.*

—News reports

We know that this God's an all-powerful God;
God's actions are not nonchalant.
We know he can punish whomever he wants.
So why be so hard on Vermont?

Yes, spending increases our deficit—sure.
Vermont, though, has not been *avant*
The rest of the country. We all spend a lot.
So why be so hard on Vermont?

Its mountains? Its hipsters? Its accent? Or what
Might tick off the Great Commandant?
We know we're all sinners; we spend and we spend.
So why be so hard on Vermont?

So by September, Bachmann, back to punt,
Was someone who had briefly been in front
But who, it was increasingly quite clear,
Would from now on be stalled more toward the rear.

Michele: A Reprise

Michele, our belle,
Things of late have truly failed to jell
For Michele.

Michele, our belle,
They're no longer buying what you sell.
Poor Michele.

Your numbers have gone in the toilet.
They say you peaked too soon.
And talking like a loon
Could not have helped a lot, although Rick
Perry does, too.

Michele, our belle,
Pundits now are bidding you farewell—
" 'Bye, Michele."

The new front-runner wasn't Romney, though.
From Texas now a mighty wind did blow.
Its smile was broad, its hair just short of stunning:
Rick Perry, who had hit the pavement running.

Enter Rick Perry

With even more impressive hair than Kerry,
At last into the race arrives Rick Perry.
Though Perry's blessed, no doubt, with splendid hair, he
Believes some things that strike some folks as scary.
Observers down in Texas still are wary.
The space beneath the hair, they say, is airy.

7.

←——→

Oops Indeed

A great campaign for Perry was projected.
In every race he'd run he'd been elected.
He did that Texas swagger to perfection,
And he was known to have a close connection
To lots of Texas money that would make
Financing his campaign a piece of cake.
And under Perry, Texas added gobs
Of what this race was most about—that's jobs.
He needed no instruction and no training
To seem at home at door-to-door campaigning.
In Iowa, he played the good ol' boy.
Compared to Mitt, he seemed the real McCoy—
A man who schmoozed and didn't seem contrived,
As if from many focus groups derived.
Conservatives considered Perry pure,
And he became the favorite du jour.

So What's with the Cowboy Boots, Rick?

You say you're the real thing from Texas —
An Aggie, not someone from Yale.
While claiming to be a straight shooter,
You plant a boot high on a bale.

'Twas cotton that grew on your farm, Rick.
You didn't grow up on the range.
No horses are used to plant cotton,
So cowboy boots seem mighty strange.

No phony? Then alter your costume.
Although they lack cowboy boots' zing,
If you have a sodbuster background,
Bib overalls might be the thing.

As nationally Rick's polling numbers soared,
The analysts who crunched the numbers scored
Him well ahead; some said he couldn't lose.
They thought once more Republicans might choose
A Texas governor at their convention,
Though Bush's name was one they'd never mention.
But Perry's chances started going south
When Perry started opening his mouth.
Debates and interviews just did him in,
For they revealed his grasp of facts was thin.

He wasn't really strong on world affairs.
He didn't seem to have a lot upstairs.
Of justices his knowledge wasn't great:
He somehow thought that there were only eight.
He thought the voting age was twenty-one.
By then, the press and bloggers had begun
To look for Perry gaffes on which to jump,
And that put Perry's numbers in a slump.
For donors, it could be a strong deflater
To watch their man Rick Perry as debater.

Rick Perry Compares Himself to Denver Broncos Quarterback Tim Tebow

When Perry discusses debates now,
He's calling himself in these rumbles
An Iowa caucuses Tebow—
Except for how often he fumbles.

The biggest gaffe had happened in November,
When Perry, in debate, could not remember
The third of three departments he would toss
Into the scrap heap once he was the boss.
Then he said "Oops." With that word it was clear
The White House was a place he'd not get near;
All three departments' workers could relax,

For he'd become the butt of comics' cracks.
He held out for a while—two months at most—
But from that moment Rick's campaign was toast.
And that left true believers with a plight:
For their crusade they didn't have a knight.

Still Looking

The far right looked for someone who'd befit
The ticket—that is, someone not named Mitt
But someone who could strongly lead the nation
Without the faintest whiff of moderation.
Chris Christie was a man they couldn't get,
And Bachmann was the quickest flopper yet.
It looked like Perry was the right's white hope,
But now they're saying Perry's just a dope.
So who will they convince now to get in?
The time is short. Their bench is looking thin.

8.

←——————→

The Search for a Mitt-Whomper

The first chance voters had to have their say
In caucuses was some two months away.
Though actual voters still had not been faced,
Some serious threats to Mitt had been erased.
Two candidates whom pundits might construe
As hurdles Romney had to jump were through.
A third campaigner who had seemed a threat,
Jon Huntsman, hadn't really caught on yet.
One problem that Jon Huntsman had to face:
He wasn't welcomed warmly by the base.
The people who thought compromise was treason
Suspected he was vulnerable to reason.
His politics and theirs were much the same,
But something troubled them about his name.
Not Huntsman, but the part just past the comma:

"Ambassador to China for Obama."
Credentials as a true Obama hater
Could not be issued; Huntsman was a traitor.
So he was not the man the right would bless
As champion to stop the Mitt Express.
The weakest candidates were those now left,
And right-wing true believers were bereft.

The Far Right Considers the Republican Front-runner

It seems that now we're stuck with Mitt.
Reciting right-wing holy writ,
He still sounds moderate, a bit.
Although it's nothing he'll admit,
A health-care plan's his biggest hit.
(The thought of that gives us a fit.)
And born-agains, from where they sit,
Still state their firm belief, to wit:
As Christians, Mormons aren't legit.
We've said for months, "This man's not it."
We wish that Palin hadn't split.
We wish that Perry weren't a nit.
(His pilot light is not quite lit.)
Because, it seems, we're stuck with Mitt.

But then, although no voting had occurred,
The order of the also-rans was stirred.
Some entertaining answers in debate
Had led Republicans to contemplate
That Herman Cain was someone they should rate
As now, perhaps, a serious candidate.
His goals before seemed simply to be these:
To have some fun and boost his speaking fees.
Like others, he said taxes should be flat,
But Cain's entire platform seemed just that.
He said we could relax. We'd all be fine
If we could just remember Nine Nine Nine.

An Inaugural Address for Herman Cain

In April, we'll all be relaxed—
All spending dough that wasn't taxed,
With Nine Nine Nine.

To working folks we'll bring enjoyment,
'Cause we'll have nearly full employment,
With Nine Nine Nine.

Our air will be pristine and clear,
And terrorists will disappear,
With Nine Nine Nine.

And scientists will find the answer
That gives the world a cure for cancer,
With Nine Nine Nine.

We'll all achieve what we endeavor,
And all of us will live forever,
With Nine Nine Nine.

A country that now seems depressed and limp'll
Be great again if we just keep things simple.

Although his patter in debates could tickle,
Cain's pool of knowledge seemed less pool than trickle.
Some questions seemed to cause his speech to vanish,
As if the questioner had asked in Spanish.
(On Libya, his silence caused a buzz:
One couldn't tell if he knew what it was.)
His ignorance, which was at times sublime,
Made Perry look like Kennan in his prime.
He never had held office in the past.
His staff was neither deep nor quick nor vast.
He spent much time, reporters kept on noting,
Promoting books in states that were not voting.
An old harassment charge had come to light.
(Cain, saying it was false, was not contrite.)
By then, as Perry's star began to fade,
Election analysts were quite dismayed

To read what they had never thought they'd read:
The Herminator now was in the lead.

The Pundits Contemplate Herman Cain

I

We've spent a month of this campaign
In trying daily to explain
The steady rise of Herman Cain.
Through willingness to risk a strain
In every muscle of the brain,
We've laid out all we think germane
To help the public ascertain
Why Cain consistently can gain
(Despite, some charge, a moral stain)
Support that doesn't seem to wane
No matter how we all complain
That thinking voters might ordain
For Cain a four-year White House reign
Is truly—to be blunt—insane.

II

So far, our work has been in vain.

His ignorance is not what did him in.
No, Cain's campaign was sabotaged by sin.

Complaints of Herman making intramural
Advances, it came out, were in the plural.
Outside the office he'd been naughty, too.
The final straw, which hastened his adieu,
Although this, too, the candidate denied:
He'd had a little something on the side.
Cain's numbers in the polls began to slip.
Then Herman Cain withdrew. He'd been a blip.
The interest in him now had run its course,
Except to see which horse he might endorse.

Lamentations of the Late-Night Comics

While Jimmy Fallon tears his hair,
Bill Maher laments, "It's just not fair."
Dave Letterman begins to pout.
They've heard that Herman Cain is out.

In common with his late-night peers,
Jon Stewart comes quite close to tears.
He'd much prefer a case of gout
To hearing Herman Cain is out.

"The man is threatening our jobs,"
Says Leno, as he softly sobs.

From Colbert tears begin to spout.
He's heard that Herman Cain is out.

They pray together, on their knees:
"Could we have Donald Trump back—please?"

9.

←——————→

Newt Redux

Cain's nod might go to Gingrich, it was said.
Yes, Gingrich, who had once been left for dead.
Improbably, he'd lived to fight again—
A star on Fox and even CNN.
Debating, Gingrich pleased the hard-right bloc—
They thought that he would clean Obama's clock—
Although the more religious folks all thought he
Had, very much like Cain, been awfully naughty.
(Both wives Newt cheated on and left were sick;
He'd shown the moral standards of a tick.)
By colleagues in the House Newt had been branded:
He'd been the only Speaker reprimanded.
He'd always found consistency constricting—
A man about whom there was no predicting.
So instantly the pooh-bahs fairly shouted
That choosing Newt could get the party routed.

Who knew if everyone had heard the last
Embarrassment in such a checkered past?
What lunacy could possibly induce
The folks to choose a cannon quite that loose?
With all his faults, which backers would admit,
Newt's great appeal was this: He wasn't Mitt.

Newt's Surge

The people who want anyone but Mitt
Now say, in desperation, Newt is it.
Yes, Newt's astute—a crafty wheeler-dealer.
His baggage, though, would fill an eighteen-wheeler.

Republicans who knew Newt from the House
Might call reporters whom they knew and grouse
About how lame as Speaker Gingrich was,
But, still, the grassroots voters were abuzz
With sharp debating points that he would score
And how he won the House in '94.
They loved it when he dissed the mainstream media
While spewing facts—a live encyclopedia.
They loved it when quite eloquent he'd wax
Or wound poor Mitt with shrewd, sarcastic cracks.
They brushed off all the right-wing commentariat,
Which treated Newt like Judas—yes, Iscariot!

("Vainglorious," said Will. To be concise,
The Joe of *Morning Joe* said, Newt's not nice.)
"A brawler's what we want," the folks would cheer.
"A guy who'll gouge and maybe bite an ear.
The hatred of Obama that we've felt
Needs someone who will hit below the belt.
Our animus requires someone bad—
No matter if he's sleazy or a cad."
New Hampshire's largest paper had provided
A lift for Newt, with whose campaign it sided.
So now the polls produced another stunner,
With Newt, the fourth un-Mitt to be front-runner.
As he passed Mitt in polls, Newt said that he
Was confident he'd be the nominee.
Like Churchill or De Gaulle, he had been called.
The men who run the party were appalled.

The Perils of the Front-runner in a Horse Race

Though Romney was leading right out of the gate,
He's also a guy some conservatives hate.
But all other entries they managed to find
Were scratched from the start or have fallen behind.
So now they've decided that Newt is a whiz—
The horse that they're backing, corrupt as he is.
Thus Gingrich, now galloping (though he's quite husky),
May make Romney look like the late Edmund Muskie.

A Pause for Prose

Callista Gingrich, Aware That Her Husband Has Cheated On and Then Left Two Wives Who Had Serious Illnesses, Tries Desperately to Make Light of a Bad Cough

Newt looked into the room where Callista had been trying to nap. "I don't like the sound of that cough," he said.

"What cough is that?" Callista replied. At that moment, she felt a cough coming on, but she managed to suppress it, emitting instead an extended beeping sound.

"The cough that's kept you in bed for the past three days," Newt said.

"It's just a little cold, Newt," Callista said. "I feel fine. Look at my hair; it's still perfectly in place. This couldn't be anything serious."

"I don't know about that," Newt said. "I hear there's a lot of dengue fever going around." He walked to the nightstand to get the thermometer.

"I'm sure that I don't have dengue fever, Newt," Callista said. "A cough is not associated with dengue fever. I haven't had the high fever. I haven't had the characteristic rash."

Newt paused as Callista, trying desperately not to cough, made a sound that suggested a motorbike that won't start. "Why is it that you know so much about dengue fever?" he asked. "Do you have reason to believe that you have dengue fever?"

"Newt," Callista said. There was a seriousness in her tone that made him stop short.

"Newt," she repeated. "You wouldn't leave me if I had dengue fever, would you? It's not a life-threatening illness."

"Well, in certain cases, complications can lead to . . ." Newt let the sentence hang.

"Newt," Callista said, in that same serious tone. "Have you found another?"

Newt looked offended. "I am appalled that you would have the nerve to ask me that question. Asking that question is as close to despicable as anything I can imagine."

" 'Close to!' " Callista said, sitting up in bed so abruptly that a single strand of her hair dislodged itself with a crack and fell over her forehead. "Did you say 'close to'? Have you been cheating on me, Newt?"

"I am leaving you, Callista," Newt said. "I have found another. I am converting to her religion—Swedenborgianism."

"You're leaving me for a Swedenborgian because you think I may have dengue fever? You're leaving a sick wife for the third time? You're converting for the third time? Won't those evangelical wackos you're trying to appeal to think that—"

"No, they won't," Newt said, cutting her off. "It turns out that they don't care at all." As he strode from the room, he heard the sound of loud coughing.

10.

←——→

Carpet Bombing

In Iowa, the caucuses unfold
In weather that's invariably cold.
To listen to long speeches is your duty.
And getting there could freeze off your patootie.
The voters who are willing to go through
This process tend to be those Christians who
Are quite convinced that Jesus wants them to;
To them the caucus seat's another pew.
On social issues these folks are the crew
To whose views candidates must tightly hew.
Those views are views that candidates rehearse
So they don't stray from chapter or from verse.
Though Hawkeye demographics weren't Mitt's best,
The caucuses were deemed a worthwhile test.
But with that test not many weeks away,
The un-Mitt Newton Gingrich still held sway.

Debates, though, were where Gingrich had excelled;
As caucus time approached, debates weren't held,
So Newt no longer was the grand enchanter,
With show-off smart remarks and flashy banter.
Then Romney's PACs put into gear their plan,
And carpet-bombing ads on Newt began.
They searched out every way that Newt was sleazy.
With Newt, of course, that sort of search was easy.
His influence, ads said, had been for sale;
He'd cashed in on a monumental scale.
One focus of the ads' sustained attack
Was money he'd received from Freddie Mac.

Newt Gingrich as Freddie Mac's $25,000-a-Month Historian

Lambasting pols who got too close to Freddie,
Newt failed to say that he himself already
Got Freddie payments that were large and steady.

But Newt said that he'd never ever lobby.
Could that mean when he seemed to do a job, he
Was doing it as more or less a hobby?

The heated jabs began to turn Newt blistery.
He said Mac's payments were for doing history.
Why Freddie needed history's a mystery.

With millions spent on TV ads by PACs,
Mitt stood apart from negative attacks—
Though once, while momentarily speaking plain, he
Referred to his opponent, Newt, as "zany."
(Rick Perry's crowd outspent Mitt in the state,
Not realizing it was just too late.)
The ads kept on, no matter what the cost
And soon the Gingrich polling lead was lost.
In Iowa, in fact, poor Newt was trounced.
A squeaker win for Romney was announced
As votes were tallied from this quirky forum.
And second place? Not Newt, but Rick Santorum.
(He'd won, some pundits thought, a special bounty
For taking his campaign to every county.)
And Newt, in a humiliating fall,
Had finished fourth, quite far beyond Ron Paul.
Conceding, Newt was somewhat less than gracious.
In fact, he sounded more and more pugnacious.
Congratulating all except for Mitt,
Whom he called moderate, well knowing it
To be an insult worse than any other—
Equivalent to slurring someone's mother.
For change, he said, just he could show the way,
And Mitt could only "manage the decay."
Some thought that Newt, now short of staff and dough,
Would have to face the facts and finally go.
Would Thatcher quit? Would Hannibal take flight?
The Newtster said that he would stay and fight.

Newt Lays Into Mitt

It's "pious baloney." Yes, pious baloney.
What Mitt speaks, Newt says, is remarkably phony:
His outsider citizen pose is all hooey;
He's hungered for office like Thomas E. Dewey.
And what he had done all those years spent at Bain
Was not create jobs but cause working stiffs pain.
While Newt covers Mitt's smooth exterior with blotches,
Obama's campaign staff just carefully watches.

11.

←——→

Stuck Again

If Romney had two triumphs in a row,
It might be hard denying him Big Mo.
New Hampshire was a course Mitt liked to play;
A rout, some said, could put this thing away.
So, making the conclusion less foregone
Meant one thing to competitors: pile on.
Rick Perry (dead man walking) said the culture
Of Bain resembled just one bird: a vulture.
But Gingrich was best suited for this strife—
Experienced in how to wield the knife.
Newt's script was gouge and butt; that's how he'd written it.
If he'd been near an ear he might have bitten it.

An Explanation of Gingrich's Ad Accusing Romney of Being Able to Speak French

Big Mo is what Gingrich is desperate to stop.
He talks of how Romney will flip and will flop—
Yes, flipping and flopping in so many ways,
He once was pro-choice and a friend of the gays.
Mitt hides that in business, wherever he'd roam,
Some innocent workers would lose hearth and home.
There's no way, Newt says, you can call Mitt a mensch.
But what's even worse is the man can speak French.

Yes, being bilingual is truly *de trop*.
The voters' reward is for what you *don't* know.
Bilingual means speaking one language too many.
We've voted for leaders who hardly speak any.
Republican voters know one thing. It's this:
That ignorance rocks. (It's sometimes called bliss.)
So all Romney-huggers should undo their clench.
Mitt Romney's a menace: The man can speak French.

Said Mitt: I'm not the man whom they've depicted.
But many Romney wounds were self-inflicted.
In talking and debating, one Mitt glitch
Was sounding very much like Richie Rich.
So often did this slip into his pitch
'Twas like a bite he simply had to itch—

The ten grand he told Perry that he'd bet,
His friendship with the NASCAR owners set,
The way he values firing so much.
His rivals said, "The man is out of touch."

Romney Says He's Not Concerned About the Poor

The remark about the poor immediately became cataloged in a growing list of awkward comments by Mr. Romney.

—*The New York Times*

His profile's divine,
His shoes have a shine;
They're almost as shined as his hair.
And voters ignore
That seeking Mitt's core
Has failed because nothing is there.

So Mitt's way ahead.
The pundits have said
That Newt might be almost kaput.
But Mitt still might lose
If he puts those shoes
Much more in his mouth with his foot.

At retail politics, we'd seen no more
Ham-handed candidate since Albert Gore.
Without the common touch that was, say, Truman's,
Mitt didn't seem quite comfortable with humans.
His small talk with the citizens appeared
To be not only very small but weird—
Weird facts, with no connection, in his chatter,
And questions to which answers didn't matter.

A Pause for Prose

President Romney Meets Other World Leaders at His First G-8 Summit

When Mitt Romney introduces himself to voters, he has a peculiar habit of guessing their age or nationality, often incorrectly. (A regular query: "Are you French Canadian?")

When making small talk with locals, he peppers the conversation with curious details. . . . Mr. Romney has developed an unlikely penchant for trying to puzzle out everything from voters' personal relationships to their ancestral homelands. . . . Mr. Romney likes to congratulate people. For what, exactly, is not always clear.

THE NEW YORK TIMES, DECEMBER 28, 2011

The moment President Romney entered the room where the opening reception was being held, he was approached by a man who shook hands and said, "*Je suis* François Hollande."

"Are you of French Canadian origin?" President Romney said, smiling broadly.

"I am French," Hollande replied, looking somewhat puzzled. "I am, in fact, the President of France."

"Congratulations," President Romney said. "Lipstick contains a substance made from fish scales."

Before Hollande could reply—in fact, before he could think of anything to say on the subject of lipstick manufacturing—they were approached by Angela Merkel, of Germany, who looked eager to greet the newest member of the G-8. President Romney peered at her briefly and then said to Hollande, "Your aunt? Your mother?"

"This is Angela Merkel, Chancellor of the Federal Republic of Germany," Hollande said.

Chancellor Merkel looked somewhat taken aback at being mistaken for Hollande's aunt. When she had regained her composure, she said to President Romney, "I know you will have much to add on the question of the debt crisis in the euro zone, Mr. President."

President Romney looked the German chancellor up and down. "I'd say you'd go about one-forty, give or take five pounds," he said. "Am I in the ballpark?"

Chancellor Merkel, hoping she might have misunderstood the President, said, "I believe the future of the euro will dominate our discussions in the coming days."

"The city that has more bridges than any other city in the world is Pittsburgh, Pennsylvania," President Romney said. "Congratulations."

"Congratulations to Pittsburgh?" Chancellor Merkel asked.

President Romney thought for a moment. "No," he said. "Just congratulations."

Stephen Harper, the Prime Minister of Canada, joined the group and introduced himself to President Romney.

"Are you of French Canadian origin?" President Romney said.

"No, I'm not," the Prime Minister replied. "But I am Canadian."

"The state stone of Michigan is the Petoskey stone," the President said. Then, spotting a gentleman standing a few feet away, he asked, "Are you of French Canadian origin?"

"No, I am David Cameron, the Prime Minister of the United Kingdom," the man said.

President Romney looked at Cameron and then at Harper and then at Cameron again. "Brothers?" he said. "Cousins? Uncle and aunt?"

"No," Cameron said.

At that point, the group was joined by Prime Minister Yoshihiko Noda, of Japan. He and President Romney were introduced. "What are you—around fifty-five or sixty?" the President asked. "Am I close?"

"I am fifty-six years of age," the Japanese Prime Minister said, rather formally.

"Yoshihiko sounds French Canadian," the President said. "I don't suppose you're of French Canadian origin, are you?"

"No, I am not," the Prime Minister said.

"Congratulations," the President replied. "Saul Rogovin, of the Detroit Tigers, hit a grand-slam home run in 1950, and it wasn't until 2008 that another Jewish pitcher hit a grand-slam home run."

"Congratulations," Chancellor Merkel said.

"Yes," the others murmured. "Congratulations."

12.

←———→

Unstuck

So from New Hampshire, Mitt left bruised and battered.
But, still, he'd won—won big—and that's what mattered.
The polls in Carolina showed that he
Was on his way to winning number three.
And Newt? The Newtster'd finished fourth again.
He couldn't capture one vote out of ten.
Mitt's team had thought that lack of cash might mean
That Newt would now retire from the scene.
That might have taken place except for this:
Newt through the years was not at all remiss
At cultivating wealthy people who
Might share with him a certain point of view,
And, conscious of the favors he might render,
Might also share some serious legal tender.
One Sheldon Adelson found in his heart
The urge to share five million as a start.

(The gambling dens he'd managed to expand
Had given him a lot of cash on hand.)

Adelson

*(Sung by Newt Gingrich supporters to the tune of "Edelweiss,"
from* The Sound of Music*)*

Adelson, Adelson,
Your donations do cheer him.
We who root
For our Newt
Smile whenever you schmeer him.

Absent your vow
That you would endow
Newt, despite his clay feet,
Adelson, Adelson,
Newt would be back on K Street.

On this there was no way to be mistaken:
Shel Adelson had saved the Newtster's bacon.
So Gingrich, fattened up with Sheldon's cash,
Became the candidate who liked to trash
Poor Mitt for everything he'd done at Bain
That caused those simple working people pain.

Mitt called such talk a weapon of the left.
Then he himself increased the issue's heft
When asked about his tax returns by saying
He'd rather not reveal what he'd been paying.
When finally he then released just one,
The damage, self-inflicted, had been done.
The Adelson donations had borne fruit:
A double-digit victory for Newt.
The certainty of Mitt had been debunked.
He hadn't just been beaten; he'd been skunked.
From Iowa, another bubble'd burst:
A recount showed Santorum finished first.
So Mitt had not won three tests in a row,
But one, which left a long, long row to hoe.

Two Attempts to Explain the Resurrection of Newt Gingrich

I

Yes, Newt appeared dead at least twice.
If Mitt's guys were playing it smart,
They would have made certain of that
By driving a stake through his heart.

II

But Newt might have said, if they had,
Proceed, Mitt. You'll see I won't mind it.

> You're free to drive stakes through my heart,
> Except that you'll first have to find it.

So now, because of one man's intervention,
A free-for-all could last through the convention.
The party leaders, who had hoped to see
Smooth sailing to select their nominee,
Now wondered why they'd all been so delighted
With what came out of Citizens United.

13.

←——————→

Anybody Out There
Want to Be President?

The party's old establishment was stunned
To see that Mitt by Newt had been outgunned.
Their horror at the thought of Gingrich grew;
For fall, the Newtster simply wouldn't do.
And thus the party's pooh-bahs' breath was bated,
In hopes they'd get Mitt rehabilitated
In Florida, which many of them guessed
Would prove to be the most important test.
The pooh-bahs called in all their reinforcements
To furnish Mitt with dazzling endorsements.
For every stalwart heaping Mitt with praise
Another one recalled with groans Newt's days
As Speaker, and said Newt as nominee
Meant losing Congress—that they'd guarantee.

Mitt Romney Responds to a Rude Awakening

I thought it was done. I thought I had won.
I felt my campaign on a roll.
But that wasn't true. Some say that I'm through.
They say what I'm lacking is soul.

But I can adapt. At that I've been apt.
I'll have much more soul than Gauguin.
We'll buy it or rent or simply invent.
My staff's coming up with a plan.

The base, though, thought no matter how you try
To change Mitt he could never be their guy.
They simply saw no way you could adjust him
Enough to make it possible to trust him.
How could you trust a man who once had said he
Was, when it came to gays, far left of Teddy?
As governor he'd sold as quite ideal
The very health plan he would now repeal.
He spoke the lines. He played his right-wing part.
But, still, they wondered, is it from the heart?
They also thought that it would be quixotic
To nominate a man quite that robotic.
They said, "We wonder if a plea, a prayer, a wish'll
Produce someone who's less, well, artificial."
Yes, even prior to Newt's stunning spurt,

Republicans were willing to assert
That they considered it an awful shame
That better players wouldn't play the game.

Wisdom from On High

Mitch Daniels should jump in, Bill Kristol cries.
That's what *The Weekly Standard* would advise.
Though at this stage this comes as a surprise,
Bill gave us Palin, so he must be wise.

They clung to hoping someone who'd declined
To run might be convinced to change his mind.
They thought that Jeb or Daniels or Paul Ryan
Or Christie could defeat that faux Hawaiian.
Some right-wing flesh and blood was what they sought,
But all their desperate efforts were for naught.
Despite their plaintive pleas, their prayers, their scolding,
They had to play the hand that they were holding.

Desperate Entreaties

On knees they plead, with both eyes misty,
For Ryan, Daniels, Bush, or Christie.

They pray into the race they'll push
Chris Christie, Ryan, Mitch, or Bush.

They see the party led to Zion
By Christie, Daniels, Bush, or Ryan.

They can't believe that this is it.
Can it be true they're stuck with Mitt?

Then Florida damped down this white-knight talk,
For Romney won, and won it in a walk.
He captured nearly half of all votes cast.
Some thought Mitt Romney had Big Mo at last.
And Newt? His message failed to resonate,
And he'd seemed somewhat passive in debate.
The Newt campaign could not gain any traction,
Not even with the right-wing tea-bag faction.
Despite a second hit of Sheldon's jack,
Newt couldn't match Mitt's negative attack.
When he complained Mitt's crowd was out of line, he
Increasingly could sound a little whiny.
What worried those who'd put their hopes on Newt
Was that he might run out of Sheldon's loot.
Such worries in the Mitt camp were unknown:
Mitt had a bunch of Sheldons of his own.

14.

Unstuck?

Was Florida to be Mitt Romney's peak?
His dominance had lasted one short week.
In February, on a single day,
Three votes were held, and none went Romney's way.
Missouri, Minnesota, Colorado
Had cast on Romney's men a cheerless shadow,
Just when they'd thought the Mittster might break free.
A single candidate had won all three
State caucuses, which caused Mitt's team to fret
That once again they faced a serious threat.
The victories that now made Mitt's men wary
Were won by Rick—Santorum, not Rick Perry.
Rick's prospects from the start had not been great.
His win in Iowa had come too late
To change the view from early in the season
That he was plodding on for no good reason.

He'd lost his Senate seat in quite a rout.
He lacked big bucks, and when he spoke about
Morality, his holy tone suggested
The Boy Scout in your troop whom you detested.
The sweater vests he wore were sometimes mocked.
But one group thought that Rick Santorum rocked:
The right-wing-social-issues-Christian crowd
Loved Rick, and from the start said they were proud
That what you heard when he gave campaign speeches
Was what you got: he lives the life he preaches.
He goes to church. His kids are schooled at home.
Unlike so many pols, he doesn't roam.
They liked it that those vests were not designer.
They liked it that his grandpa was a miner.
They saw a true believer in Santorum.
(His family they saw as ad valorem.)
Abortion of all kinds, of course, he'd banish.
He'd like both birth control and gays to vanish.
He thinks our nation's founders from the start
Had not meant church and state to be apart.
What JFK would have us all believe
On church and state, Rick said, just made him heave.
The problem that Rick's fandom faced had been
They couldn't see a way that he could win.
Santorum, dogged man in sweater vests,
Had now won fully half of all the tests.
So now they started thinking that he could
Bring victory for purity and good.

We Pick Rick

(A Santorum campaign song, sung to the tune of "We Like Ike," by Irving Berlin)

We pick Rick.
Yes, Rick's with whom we will stick.
He's the guy
All over whom we're swarming.

We pick Rick.
Though some imply he's a hick.
He well knows
There is no global warming.

He'll say on CNN
The sins that we must smother.
And he can keep those men
From marrying each other.

We pick Rick
'Cause he'll tell liberals real quick
What God says
No matter if they're willing:
Abortion's baby killing.
So we pick Rick.

Some flare-ups of the ancient culture wars
Helped Rick put on the board those stunning scores.
When contraception funding raised a row,
The average voter had to wonder how
Some people at this stage still didn't know
That this was settled fifty years ago.
But some Rick voters thought—make no mistake—
That freedom of religion was at stake,
That sacred values might be cast aside.
A war on women, Democrats replied,
Was what the right wing now was waging.
And soon, of course, the two sides were engaging
In fights on who was truly church defender
And who oppressor of the female gender.

Contraception (of All Things)

Republicans are bashing birth control,
As candidates far-rightward scurry.
The voters haven't heard such talk in years.
We're going backwards in a hurry.

A Pause for Prose

Rick Santorum Takes a Turn at Homeschooling

The Santorum children were relieved to hear their father announce that the next hour would be devoted to American history. They were tired of talking about sex all the time. That morning's biology lesson had been about how contraception can cause diseases such as St. Vitus Dance and Housemaid's Knee. Two separate field trips that week had been to the worst slums in Washington, in order to demonstrate how sex for purposes other than procreation will almost invariably lead to drug addiction, depravity, poverty, and homelessness. In the third hour of the second trip, while being shown how drunken derelicts were driven to look for food in a dumpster, little Kevin Santorum had looked up to his father and said, "Why can't we take field trips to the water treatment plant like other kids?"

Beginning the American history lesson, Senator Santorum said, "The framers of our Constitution, such as Thomas Jefferson, were Christians who had no intention of driving people of faith from the public square. They did not intend the United States to have absolute separation of church and state. As we learned in Personal Health class earlier this week, absolute separation of church and state can make a person want to throw up."

Kevin raised his hand and was recognized by his father. "My friend Timmy Burnside says that Thomas Jefferson was in favor of what he called a wall separating church and state," Kevin said. "Timmy says that 'separation of church and state' is actually Jefferson's term. That's what Timmy says."

For a while, Senator Santorum said nothing, but his expression was stern. His cheeks had grown flushed. Kevin, made uneasy by the silence, decided to break it with another question: "So, did Thomas Jefferson throw up all the time?"

Their father still hadn't spoken. He looked angry. Finally, he said, "Timmy is inhabited by Satan."

"Timmy Burnside?" Kevin said.

"Yes, Timmy Burnside."

"The Timmy Burnside who lives down the street?"

"That's right," Senator Santorum said. "I don't want you to play with Timmy Burnside anymore."

"But Dad," Kevin said. "Timmy Burnside has a Wii with both Mario Super Sluggers and Madden NFL 12—my two favorite games."

"Those whom Satan would inhabit he first tempts," the Senator said.

"So then could we get Mario Super Sluggers and Madden NFL 12 for our Wii?" Kevin asked.

"Absolutely not," Senator Santorum said. "In fact, there will be no more playing with the Wii. We're giving away the Wii. It is Satan's tool and is thus unclean to the touch."

There was an audible groan from the children. "Leave it to Kevin to ruin everything," one of the older kids whispered to his sister. "He should know that it's always safer to talk about sex."

15.

Carpet Bombing Redux

What happens when a threat to Mitt arrives?
The Mitt campaign calls out B-25s.
The bombs begin. And there is rarely trouble
Reducing a competitor to rubble.
As senator, they argued, Rick was tending
Toward earmarks, not to speak of pork barrel spending.
Yes, Rick, according to what Mitt's team aired,
Was nice enough but not, in fact, prepared
To hold the highest office in the land,
With actual bombers under his command.
Destroying opposition was the way
That Mitt's team saw for him to win each fray,
Because the base's trust still stood unearned.
Mitt still talked right-wing talk like lines he'd learned.
As governor, he told one crowd quite clearly,
His thrust had been conservative — "severely."

Severely

(To the tune of the Moonglows' "Sincerely," or "America the
*   Beautiful," depending on who's singing.)*

Severely. Yes, I governed severely.
Uh-uh, I wasn't nearly
A moderate then.

Severely. Yes, I governed severely.
I moved further right yearly—
Right-wing way back when.

I swear, I can't fathom just how
That health-care law got through.
And with my name, too. Repealing such a law's the first
   thing I will do.

Severely. Yes, I governed severely.
And I governed austerely.
I'll do it again.

The race now had a different complexion.
In Michigan, the primary election
Would be on February's final day.
The Romney carpet bombers bombed away.
This testing ground was Romney's home state, too.
(Though he of course had homes in quite a few.)
If Romney failed to win his home state vote,

It might for Mitt, they said, be all she wrote.
His casual talk was still quite far from supple.
He mentioned Ann owned Cadillacs—"a couple."
He loved not just the cars here, Romney said.
But how high trees extend above one's head.

I Thought That I Would Never See
a Pol Who Loved the Height of Trees

I love this state. It seems right here. The trees are the
right height.

> —Mitt Romney, in his home state of Michigan

Away from here, I find no trees that please—
No trees at such a perfect height as these.
For me, I cannot ever be at ease
With trees that grow no higher than one's knees
Or too-tall trees that splinter in a freeze.
Wisconsin, sure, has bragging rights on cheese,
And California's rich in Cantonese,
And Colorado's where to take your skis.
Connecticut, of course, has Lyme disease.
At none of these am I prepared to sneeze.
But here we have the perfect height of trees.

I know that I will never see a sight
As lovely as a tree whose height is right.

Santorum, too, seemed terribly hard put
To keep himself from shooting toward his foot.
From Catholics he received a strong rebuke
For saying JFK's speech made him puke.
His hectoring on things like birth control
Had gotten shrill enough to try the soul.
Those views, the feeling went, among some others,
Would in the fall offend suburban mothers.
The base, though, still could not commit to Mitt.
Mitt simply wouldn't be a perfect fit.
Republicans for once began to mention
The snarl that could occur at their convention.
Was Mitt a candidate so mediocre
That they might need the service of a broker?

16.

Stuck Again

So Romney won his home state vote—but barely.
Republicans now faced the fact that rarely,
If ever, had the word "presumptive" come
And gone so many times as in this scrum.
One moment Romney seems to have the prize—
The delegates, endorsements from the guys
Who've always in the party had the clout.
A moment later something casts a doubt
On whether in November he'd come through.
That starts anew: in lieu of Romney, who?
Some longed still for some sort of alpha lion—
A pro like Christie, Daniels, Bush, or Ryan.
In Michigan, Newt finished fourth once more,
Which meant, some thought, that he'd be out the door.
The right-wing forces thought that they would do
Much better fielding just one man, not two.

When Gingrich had a major surge, he'd tried
Suggesting Rick Santorum move aside,
Which would, by Newton's reckoning, permit
The right-wing vote for once to be unsplit.
At that point, Rick would not accept defeat.
Nor now would Newt, when shoes had changed their feet.

On Not Leaving the Field

Right-wingers who want to be heard
Note Newt at his best's only third.
But if right-wing votes were combined,
The front-runner might fall behind.
So they say to Newt, "Won't you go?"
And Newt, being Newt, answers no.

Newt's ideological kin
Are dreading a moderate's win.
They argue they might turn the tide
If Gingrich will just step aside.
Then Mitt can't divide a duet.
And Newt, being Newt, still says *nyet*.

"When England was under the blitz,
Did Churchill say, 'Let's call it quits'?"
Says Newt, "That is not what you see
From statesmen like Churchill and me."

> "Oh, please, just this once, Newt," they say.
> And Newt, being Newt, says "No way."

If Mitt had hoped to have "presumptive" nailed
On Super Tuesday, then of course he failed.
In delegates his total acquisition
Was not enough to crush the competition.
Sure, Rick, who'd won three states, was still behind;
Just Georgia had the Newtster on its mind.
But still Mitt failed to get the votes he needed
To briskly march toward Tampa unimpeded.
And if he finally managed his ascendance,
Would he be too far right for independents?
His manager said no, this wasn't true,
Because, like Etch A Sketch, he'll start anew.
To start anew—to flop, then flip—appeared
To be precisely what the right wing feared.
Yes, added to accumulated fodder, it
Portrayed him as a Massachusetts moderate—
The sort of man who, once he wins the bid'll,
With just one shake, skedaddle toward the middle.

The Situation

So Mitt's officially an Etch A Sketch,
And Rick says JFK's speech made him retch.
Ron Paul's a ditz, and Gingrich is a letch.
Though nets are flung as far as they will stretch,
There isn't any white knight there to fetch.
Republicans thus sit around and kvetch.

17.

←—————→

The Southern Strategy

In Southern states, Mitt Romney's stump routine
Was singular, and something to be seen.
To come off even folksier than Paul,
He'd throw in, now and then, a goofy "y'all."
His favorite food? He sounded as if it's
Some catfish with a side of "cheesy grits."
Some Southerners thought Mitt should quit pretending;
From him, it came across as condescending
To think with Southern voters he'd be blending
By dropping *g* from every gerund's ending.
As if he had some chaw in his jeans pocket,
He stood there and recited "Davy Crockett."
The Southern crowd just wondered what it means
That he had perfect creases in those jeans.

I'm a Mandarin Who's Panderin'

Mitt Romney's my name.
I'm aimin' to please.
The floor at my feet
Is littered with *g*'s.

Three Southern contests happened on one day.
A sweep, Newt thought, would certainly convey,
Considering his two already won,
That his Old South possessed a favorite son.
The logic of that no one could dispute.
The problem was the son's name wasn't Newt:
Yes, Hat Trick Rick Santorum had once more
With Gingrich and with Romney wiped the floor.
He only had a week, though, to enjoy
That victory, and then came Illinois.
Mitt triumphed there, and in Wisconsin, too.
Could there be any more he had to do?
The anyone-but-Mitt folks grew less raucous.
DeMint, the leader of the Wing Nut Caucus,
Endorsed Mitt, as did all the white knights who
Some hoped would jump in late and stage a coup:
The voters could no longer pull a switch
And go for Jeb or Paul or Chris or Mitch.
At last, the script that Mitt had long rehearsed
Had gone too far, most thought, to be reversed.

At last, it seemed he'd put away the game,
And had "presumptive" tacked on to his name.

The Republican National Committee Selects a Campaign Slogan

Our slogan's been chosen.
We think it's a hit.
We'll shout from the rafters,
"We've settled for Mitt!"

18.

←→

The Party's Over

Despite the many contests that he'd won,
The count of delegates could not be spun
In ways that made the plain arithmetic
Look anything but very grim for Rick.
Whatever flaws he has, the man can count.
His campaign debt had now begun to mount.
At Easter time he said he would suspend
His operation. Rick had reached the end.

Adieu Santorum

The race will miss the purity
That you alone endow.

> We'll never find another man
> Who's holier than thou.

And Newt? Would Newt continue in the fray
Now, even though he didn't have a ray?
One factor made his situation worse:
Shel Adelson was zipping up his purse.
Yes, sixteen million—not a penny more—
Turned out to be as much as Newt could schnorrer
From Adelson, who, though he'd closed Newt's drama,
Said he'd give millions more to beat Obama.
He guaranteed Republican campaigns
Would benefit from his ill-gotten gains.

End of the Line?

> *Sheldon Adelson, the Las Vegas billionaire who has been
> the biggest backer to a group supporting Newt Gingrich,
> said this week that Mr. Gingrich had reached "the end of
> his line" in his bid for the presidency.*
>
> *—The New York Times*

So Newt's coming closer to facing defeat?
His main sugar daddy's no longer so sweet.

And Newt never was: Why, when he had the power
Of all of that sugar, he still sounded sour.

So why was he remaining in the fight?
Could Newton be there simply out of spite?
Did he remain, and not just take a hike,
To bloody up a man he didn't like?
It's possible, but finally, in May,
Newt grudgingly announced he'd go away.

Newt Departs from the Island of Poliwonks
(The saddest leave-taking since Max left the Wild Things)

"Don't go!" all the poliwonks started to croon.
"What other Republican dared to harpoon
The Mittster for being a heartless tycoon?
Who's left to start planning a town on the moon,
As if he had stepped from the pages of *Dune*?
Who never did hesitate once to impugn
The press—his best foil—when it seemed opportune?
Oh why, Newt, oh why must you leave us so soon?"
But Newt, though quite portly, as well as jejune,
Just floated away, like a hot air balloon.

So it was Mitt. He'd won. The next month he
Was called "presumptive" by the RNC.
At last the last threat, Rick, had been defeated.
The sniper, Newt, had finally retreated
Back where he could fulfill Callista's dreams,
With funding from his shady K Street schemes.
The right was stuck with Mitt, so said the news.
But had Mitt now been stuck with all their views?

Small Animals Dispatched

So Mitt's finally won. The whack-a-mole's over.
The moles have been whacked, and Mitt is in clover.
The clover smells good, but here is the riddle:
Can Romney now move it a bit toward the middle?
By dropping the wacko-right banner he's gripping,
Will he be accused of more flopping and flipping?

19.

←——→

Mitt's Got the Gold

So Mitt alone emerged then from the brawl—
Opposed by none, except for Dr. Paul.
The doctor's praises hadn't gone unsung
By loyal backers, many of them young.
A libertarian, he espoused the view
That you can do whatever you can do—
Unless (and this requires some contortion)
The thing you want to do is an abortion.
In early contests, Ron Paul did quite well,
Although reporters did begin to dwell
On whether publications in the past
That bore his name were of a racist cast.
His bearing was much less than charismatic.
His views on war were downright Democratic.
His role was of the somewhat odd, erratic,
Eccentric uncle living in the attic.

So Mitt's advisers saw no cause to fret
That Paul remained. The doctor was no threat.
In fact, they thought it might be sticky wicket
If Paul broke ranks to head another ticket.
So Romney found with Paul some common ground.
The Mittster wanted Paul to stick around.

Opposites Remain

Paul has his own style, which is folksy, not canned.
Religion? He's got one. His prophet's Ayn Rand.
By Rand's eerie theories he's fervently gripped,
So he won't do flip-flops. He long ago flipped.

With Romney's lead now finally unassailable,
His team began to make him unavailable
For those occasions where the work of staff
Could not preclude the presence of a gaffe.
They skipped the gatherings where nonchalance
Could lead to an embarrassing response.
They built, at any must-attend affair,
Around their man a *cordon sanitaire*.
And interviews, which also could bring shocks,
Were not allowed — not even those on Fox.
In interviews, they'd found, their man could quickly
Become a CEO — aloof and prickly.

Mitt Romney's Handlers Devise a New Strategy

To keep him from uttering what might appall,
He'll simply be saying now nothing at all.

They wanted Mitt on message, which was this:
Obama is a man we must dismiss.
He had his opportunity to cure
The hard times that our people still endure.
We can't recover under his command.
Our system's something he can't understand,
Because the man has never had a hand
In business—that's the business of this land.
What's needed to escape recession's clenches?
A man who's been there in the business trenches,
Who, seeing an economy destroyed,
Rolls up his sleeves and gets those folks employed.

Business Experience

Last week, Mitt Romney floated an idea at a campaign rally in Las Vegas: the future president should be required to have three years of business experience before serving in office.

—The Washington Post

Experience in business is vital, said Mitt—
Three years at the least, in the plan he unveiled.
Though Truman's accomplishments seem to suggest
The business in question would have to have failed.

20.

←——→

Bain

Mitt Romney from the start had often stated
That many jobs by him had been created
In businesses that thrived throughout his reign
As founder and the CEO of Bain.
He said a hundred thousand was the total—
A number shown to be, well, anecdotal.
He dropped the number from his speeches; still,
He said a savvy businessman could fill
So many jobs now vanished since the nation
Got handicapped by overregulation.
Free enterprise, Mitt said, was the elixir
To fix this mess—and he the master fixer.
His business background was Mitt Romney's pride.
The problem was there was another side.
His rivals in the primaries rebutted:
Mitt's firm cashed in while companies were gutted.

Rick Perry was the first to brand Bain's culture
With what was quite a scary label: "vulture."
In Carolina, not to be outdone,
Newt Gingrich then had grabbed that ball and run.
With money from his Vegas sugar daddy,
He ran some ads that showed Mitt as a baddie
Who piled on riches sitting in his suite
While putting honest workers on the street.
So now the Democrats began to skewer
Mitt Romney as a business evildoer.
Their strategy seemed simple on its face.
As governor the man was no disgrace,
But what's he mostly praised for in his state?
A health plan he professes now to hate.
And so his great accomplishment was one
On which he wouldn't be allowed to run.
His business record, then, was all he had;
It's what was meant to be his launching pad.
Success in business had to be his claim.
And if that claim takes on a hint of shame—
If, when employment figures still are lagging,
He could not point to Bain to back his bragging—
He's just a guy, no matter what his spiel,
Who salvaged one Olympics—no big deal.

The Bain of Mitt Romney's Existence

He's running on all of his triumphs at Bain,
But some say the Democrats ought to refrain
From saying Bain's gain was at times inhumane
(Because of its strategy aiming to drain
A company's treasure, no matter what pain
Is caused to the workers whom it won't retain).
Yes, Bain did some good, its defenders explain:
Some pension funds shared in its capital gain.
So *vulture*'s a label for Mitt they disdain—
Though *buzzard*'s okay, and is just as germane.

Some Democrats found such attacks unfair,
But others pointed out that Bain was where
Mitt Romney said that, gathering those stocks, he
Got skills in leadership and plain old moxie—
The very skills, he says, Obama lacks.
So Bain's fair game, they said, for such attacks:
Since Bain is central to the claims Mitt's made,
We need to know just how that game was played.

21.

←——————→

The White House Prepares

Obama's team, preparing for the pending
Election, knew some fences needed mending
With groups whose backing had become lukewarm,
Because Obama's promise of reform
That he as President would carry through
Had ended up too far back in the queue.
The Dream Act hadn't passed, despite orations.
So he came close by changing regulations
To say a person (often a Latino)
Brought here illegally as a bambino,
Could go about his business and not fret
(As long as some conditions had been met)
About the chance that he could soon be thrown
From here into a land he'd never known.
Thus fences with Latinos were repaired,

And, since they thought of Mitt as gringo squared,
They could present the Democratic slate
With bigger Spanish margins than '08.
And here is what Obama had to say
That brought a cheer from people who are gay
(Although he didn't say it when he'd planned,
'Cause Biden, he of loose lips, tipped his hand):
On marriage vows, he now felt ecumenical—
So even those whose sex is quite identical
Should be allowed their separate lives to blend
And live those lives together to the end.
Before, he'd called his thoughts on this "evolving."
His statement, then, went quite a way toward solving
The beef of those who thought he'd moved too slowly.
Though those who think such unions are unholy
Were mad, the issue has no longer got
A button on it that remains red-hot.
(Opponents are much older, meaning, verily,
This issue will be settled actuarially.)

Obama on Immigration and Gay Marriage

He led among them going in,
And this, the White House thought, would lock it.
Announcements that Obama made
Put gay Latinos in his pocket.

The Dems were busy shoring up support
From women (moms and any other sort)—
Reminding them the GOP had made
A promise to repeal Roe versus Wade.
They also built the teams that had displayed
In '08 how a ground game should be played.
The teams were not the same from sea to sea.
Electoral College voting being key,
A voter's vote would hardly mean a thing
Except in states referred to now as swing.
The citizens of swing states would decide
Because of where they happen to reside.
In states where red- or blueness is conceded,
Your vote for president's not really needed.
The total vote the winner can ignore.
The total doesn't help. Just ask Al Gore.

Ohio

(A 2012 version of the Wonderful Town *classic)*

> *With the rest of the states either solidly red or solidly
> blue, the election will be decided in nine or ten swing
> states.*
>
> —*News reports*

Why oh why oh why oh?
Why did I ever leave Ohio?
Why did I locate where, since it's no swing state,

Pollsters don't trouble to track?
Zero is my vote's weight.
Reason to vote? That's what I lack.
Oh why oh why oh
Did I leave Ohio?
Maybe I better go O-H-I-O,
Where I could have my vote back.

22.

The Race Shapes Up

Though housing showed some slight signs of recovering,
The unemployment numbers still were hovering
Above a pretty dismal eight percent—
A figure causing widespread discontent.
Unless the ranks of jobless started thinning,
The President could hardly count on winning.
Obama, it was said, should just accept
The fact his policies had proved inept.
And he could only answer in reverse:
Without my actions, this would be much worse.

A Rejected Campaign Slogan

With confidence low and firms still not hiring,
"It could have been worse" is not too inspiring.

He now faced Mitt, and one opponent more:
The promise he'd portrayed four years before,
When his campaign had promised change and hope.
By now, Obama'd given up that trope.
Mitt Romney did have troubles of his own.
Withholding his returns became a bone
That newshounds chewed away on any day
There didn't seem to be much else to say.
They theorized on what he had to hide,
They wrote about reluctance to abide
By rules obeyed by everyone below
His customary rank of CEO.

Mitt Romney's Tax Returns

Demands come from left and from right.
Mitt Romney, though, says he'll sit tight.
We've given you people enough,
Says Ann, sounding suddenly tough.

Conspiracy theories abound.
Mitt's critics relentlessly pound.
Why go through this sort of ordeal?
What doesn't Mitt want to reveal?

Some shelters far off from our shore?
Well, sure, but there has to be more.
And, really, we already know
His tax rate is terribly low.
Could some corporate losses have meant
That one year he paid not a cent?
What's in there to make voters squeal?
What doesn't Mitt want to reveal?

What deed was so sleazy that he'll
So desperately try to conceal
Exposure with such stubborn zeal?
What fiddling did Romney feel
Showed even a wealthy big wheel
Who feels some gray areas' appeal
Is slippery, just like an eel?
What doesn't Mitt want to reveal?

In polls, the man the voters thought most fit
To manage the economy was Mitt;
In business Mitt had proven his agility.
He finished, though, way back in likability.
(Although, despite Obama's mass appeal, he

Could hardly be described as touchy-feely,
Most folks would to the pollsters volunteer,
"Sure, he's a guy with whom I'd have a beer.")
What voters saw in Romney was, all told,
That at his warmest he was rather cold.
They couldn't really feel enthusiastic
About a man who might be made of plastic.
Obama, also guarded as a rule,
Did not strike folks as cold; he just seemed cool.

The Likability Factor

The polls agree: President Barack Obama is likable. The question is whether he's likable enough to get re-elected.
—*Politico*

It's said, as a rule, the most likable guy
Is likely the guy who'll pull through.
And given the candidates now set to try,
The Democrats hope that is true.

Though voters, polls show, think Obama is cool
And Romney is colder than ice,
More likable's not an infallible tool.
Remember: Dick Nixon won twice.

23.

<— —>

A June Surprise

Quite late in June, the nation's highest court
Was, in its final session, to report
Its finding on Obama's health-care act.
The betting odds against the act were stacked:
When looking at the Roberts court, one saw
The sway of ideology, not law.
Though Kennedy would now and then demur,
Four right-wing justices were always sure
The right-wing course was what the Framers meant.
The liberals—four—were usually in dissent.
Not many thought the justices would say
The act was constitutionally okay.
Force purchasing by mandate! Five would glower,
And then agree no Congress has that power.

<— 103 —>

We Hate It 'Cause It's His: A Republican Sea Chantey

> *[The individual mandate had] been at the heart of Republican health-care reforms for two decades. The mandate made its political début in a 1989 Heritage Foundation brief titled "Assuring Affordable Health Care for All Americans," as a counterpoint to the single-payer system and the employer mandate, which were favored in Democratic circles. . . . The mandate made its first legislative appearance in 1993, in the Health Equity and Access Reform Today Act—the Republicans' alternative to President Clinton's health-reform bill.*
>
> *—Ezra Klein,* The New Yorker

Oh, why do we so loathe this thing?
We used to love it so.
We used to say "For health reform
This is the way to go."
We said it was free enterprise
(And we explained just how).
If this was our idea back then,
How could we hate it now?

We hate it 'cause it's his, lads. We hate it 'cause it's his.
We hate it 'cause it's his, lads. That's what our hatred is.
You needn't be a whiz, lads, to ace this simple quiz.
We hate it 'cause it's his, lads. We hate it 'cause it's his.

Surprise! John Roberts left his usual cluster.
He ruled the health law's mandate did pass muster.
Comparing health plans, it was now less credible
To say Mitt's mandate's fine since it's not federal
But this Obama plan, we know quite well,
Is sure to put us on the path to Hell.
From what some analysts could ascertain,
John Roberts made the issue less germane.
But it remained a dragon to be slain;
The act had not been demonized in vain:
The right thought Roberts' ruling on the case
Might be a way to energize the base.

A Sea Chantey Reprise

If Mitt's plan was the model here,
What caused this great upheaval?
If Mitt's makes sense, then why is this
Such socialistic evil?
If this approach once seemed so good
That all of us were for it,
Just why is it so wicked now
That all of us abhor it?

We hate it 'cause it's his, lads. We hate it 'cause it's his.
We hate it 'cause it's his, lads. That's what our hatred is.

You needn't be a whiz, lads, to ace this simple quiz.
We hate it 'cause it's his, lads. We hate it 'cause it's his.

A lull for the Olympics coincided
With what developed into a misguided
And goofy journey that Mitt took abroad,
Where by his gaffes the foreigners were awed.

Mitt Visits Foreign Lands

(And not to hide money)

The Mittster, while taking a three-nation swing
Showed talent for saying the very wrong thing.
He teed off our English friends lickety-split;
The tabloids in London Town called him a twit.
Though Mitt said his motives were never ulterior,
He seemed to be calling the Arabs inferior.
In English and Arabic venom Mitt bathed.
'Twas only in Poland he came out unscathed.
His trip, meant to show foreign policy cred,
Because of Mitt's gaffes was a model instead
Of what not to say when abroad one doth roam.
So here's the consensus: He should have stayed home.

Though pollsters said we always should remember
How much could change before we reach November,
The polls rained down, just like a summer shower,
With some poll every hour on the hour.
In almost any survey that you'd check,
Barack and Mitt were running neck and neck.
On cable, every well-connected speaker
Assured us that this race would be a squeaker.
In August, though, by pundits we were told
Mitt's team might have to make some move that's bold
If this prize was at last to go to Mitt.
The race required shaking up a bit.

24.

Shaken Up

Before "presumptive" stuck to Romney's name,
The press already played a little game
Of speculating just what Mitt might do
In choosing who would be his number two.
One measure of the candidates he'd bested:
Just one of them was seriously suggested.
Yes, Tim Pawlenty, who had been the guy
McCain had also thought that he might try
As veep before, with yardage to amass,
He switched and called that long Hail Mary pass.
The candidates who'd been in real contention
With Romney for the win received no mention.
Considering Mitt Romney's gringohood,
Some thought the veep position surely would
Be offered this time to a person who
Was plainly of a somewhat darker hue.

(They feared one day the Grand Old Party might
Just disappear if it stayed lily-white.)
There were some candidates like that available—
Non-WASP, attractive, and to voters salable.
Marc Rubio, a rising star, was floated,
And so was Nikki Haley, who'd promoted
Mitt Romney very early in her state.
And Condi Rice was mentioned for the slate.
Poor Bobby Jindal hoped that the pervading
Impression of that dorky speech was fading.

Cuisine Diversity

If Rubio, Jindal, or Haley or Rice
Got put on the ticket by Romney as vice,
Republicans possibly then could entice
Some voters who like to eat food that has spice
And not stick with voters who think that a slice
Of white bread's the food that will always suffice.

But most thought Mitt, once having heard this chatter,
Would add a slice of white bread to his platter.
Rob Portman, of Ohio, pundits guessed,
Would likely be the grail of Romney's quest.
A senator once head of OMB,
He boasted a magnificent CV.

His name for veep had also been revealed
Before McCain unleashed that bomb downfield.
Ohio was a swing state that just might,
Republicans had hoped, swing toward the right.
Ohio mattered, no two ways about it;
Republicans had never won without it.
The campaign press corps would, of course, persist
In adding politicians to the list.
McDonnell of Virginia was discussed.
Support of Christie had become robust.
And if a woman veep might have a shot,
There was some talk of Senator Ayotte.
But Portman was the favorite going in,
Though some thought Tim Pawlenty just might win.
Then, suddenly, we heard that Mitt was veering
Toward Ryan, he of social engineering—
The right-wing type. (Or that's what Newt had said—
A quip that got him taken to the shed.)
Paul Ryan was, as everyone agreed,
In some ways what a guy like Mitt would need—
A young, attractive man who'd always been
Quite human, comfortable inside his skin.
A natural who never seemed aloof, he
Could chat with folks and not say something goofy.
He'd been the darling of the tea-bag right,
A group whose love of Mitt had been quite slight.
Conservatives at last could now rejoice—
Quite heartened when they heard of Romney's choice.
And liberals, too, thought this would just be good,
Because the choice of Ryan likely would

Divert the campaign spotlight's glare
From joblessness to things like Medicare—
A battlefield Republicans don't choose,
Since it is one fight that they usually lose.

Medicare to the Forefront

*Polls show that Medicare is now the third most vital issue
of the campaign, and Paul Ryan's plan to change it is
unpopular with likely voters.*

—*News reports*

Yes, any talk of Medicare
Is almost guaranteed to scare
A lot of voters everywhere.
Though Medicare, in truth, has ne'er
Been short of signs of wear and tear—
Its funding source may need repair—
Most folks are fierce in guarding their
Entitlements, and they declare
That any change would be unfair,
Would cheat them out of their fair share.
So politicians are aware
There's always risk in going there.
They keep their distance from that snare.
You cannot win the Croix de Guerre
By meddling with Medicare.

Your fate's more likely to compare
To agonizing *mal de mer,*
A bad encounter with a bear,
A trip to the electric chair.
So talk of Medicare is rare,
But Ryan's put it in the air,
And some Republicans despair.

Mitt's team, though, countered with an ad
That said Obama's health-care project had
Robbed Medicare of billions, which, for sure,
Would go right to the undeserving poor.
Though that, in fact, was not exactly true,
The ad had done what it was meant to do:
The deficit on Medicare Mitt faced
Apparently was gradually erased.
Still, Ryan's budget Democrats would pitch
As taking from the poor to help the rich.
One portrait for which liberals saw him posing:
A banker who stays cheerful while foreclosing,
A follower, in pictures they would paint,
Of Ayn Rand, Gordon Gekko's patron saint.

Ayn Rand
(Sung to the tune of "Blue Moon")

Ayn Rand,
Because of you I'm now free.
Because of what you have taught,
I know it's all about me.

Ayn Rand,
You taught we should be ambitious,
And strive to be avaricious,
Since money's truly delicious.

And we shouldn't share a nickel of this money
With citizens who can't prevail.
The government is not the Easter Bunny.
The poor are weaklings who deserved to fail.

Ayn Rand,
Before you I was immobile.
Because of you I now know
That being selfish is noble.

25.

←→

Money Makes the World Go Around

The main campaign, declared those in the know,
Was bound to cost an awful lot of dough.
In Citizens United, the Supremes
Had ruled (by five to four, of course) that schemes
Called Super PACs could (sticking to a role
Not subject to a candidate's control)
Spend millions to destroy his rival's name
And thus essentially control the game.
Yes, buying pols, no matter what the price,
Was simply speech—free speech, to be precise.
By summer, Sheldon Adelson was seen
As one iconic figure of this scene.

Sheldon Adelson's Free Speech

*Casino mogul Sheldon Adelson is on the brink of reaching
$71 million in contributions thus far in this election cycle.*
—Roll Call

Yes, money is speech, so the Court has decreed.
While Adelson thinks this is splendid,
The rest of us wonder, as cash calls the tune,
Is this what the Framers intended?

Shel Adelson had speech more like a shout,
With millions spent to get Obama out.
Newt's old enabler had upped his bet
That, digging in the deepest pockets yet,
He'd get a government that he could praise
For following the wisdom of his ways.
There had been talk that that's precisely how
Things worked out well for Sheldon in Macao.
But Yanks are also willing to kowtow
As long as they can milk a big cash cow:
In Israel, Shel showed Mitt to his friends,
Like showing off a new Mercedes-Benz.

Sheldon and Mitt's Beautiful Adventure

So someone more hard-line than any Likudnik—
Yes, someone who's thought of as mostly a nudnik—
Can show up escorting the number one guy.
It just goes to show you what money can buy.

And Ryan, within days of his selection,
Flew off to Vegas to express affection
For Adelson, who'd greatly stretched his reach
By giving all those millions of free speech.
And who'd step in if Sheldon should go broke?
Those black-tie populists, the brothers Koch.
The Democrats had fat cats of their own,
Although the President had not been prone
To give big donors what they're always needing:
Some ego stroking and much care and feeding.
With heated words and even some derision
He'd criticized the Super PAC decision.
And now he'd have to sing a different song,
And ask for cash for what he'd said was wrong.
Because of that, perhaps, he'd been quite slow
Approving use of Super PAC big dough.
The analysts all said that wasn't smart,
Surrendering to Romney such a start.

The super-rich would mainly fund this race,
And some said we had now become a place
Where billionaires decide. The only test
Is which side can persuade them to invest.

A Pause for Prose

No Coordination, No Communication

INTERVIEWER: Your Super PAC, America the Super, has now spent just over three million dollars on negative television ads attacking Art Schwartz, the most serious opponent of Jeff Gold in the race for the Senate, and—with all due respect, ma'am—that has naturally raised questions about how closely America the Super is connected to the Gold campaign.

SUPER PAC CEO: By law, a candidate's campaign cannot coordinate or communicate with a Super PAC. America the Super is for America being super. If that leads to calling for an investigation into whether Mr. Schwartz did any inappropriate touching when he was a scoutmaster in 1978—because a lot of those scoutmasters did, you know—so be it.

INTERVIEWER: Well, you do understand the assumption some have that there might be more contact than the spirit of the law intends there to be, given your closeness with Mr. Gold.

SUPER PAC CEO: My closeness? What do you mean by my closeness?

INTERVIEWER: Because you're, well, his—

SUPER PAC CEO: Because I'm his mother?

INTERVIEWER: Well, yes, because you're his mother. Because you're his mother, it's natural for people to assume that the two of you often talk—

SUPER PAC CEO: He never calls. He never writes.

INTERVIWER: Well, let's take the thirty-second ads that America the Super made accusing Mr. Schwartz of having attended a summer session at Harvard—ads that started airing the morning after Mr. Gold made the original Harvard accusation, famously brandishing a copy of Mr. Schwartz's transcript during a television debate. Is it your contention that you and Mr. Gold did not discuss—

SUPER PAC CEO: Discuss! Discuss! How can you discuss something with someone who never calls his own mother?

INTERVIEWER: So you're saying that the Super PAC runs completely independently, with no instructions from Mr. Gold?

SUPER PAC CEO: Discuss! Discuss! I could have a heart attack— God forbid—and be lying on the floor. Supine! Do you think he'd know? He'd never know. By law, a Super PAC cannot coordinate or communicate with a candidate's campaign.

INTERVIEWER: And you haven't phoned him?

SUPER PAC CEO: I should phone and be told by some snippy little secretary that he's busy? I should phone and be put on hold until next *Tish B'ov*? I should phone and be told that, by law, a Super PAC cannot coordinate or communicate with a candidate's campaign? Please. Spare me. Let an old woman die in peace.

INTERVIEWER: Then you're ill?

SUPER PAC CEO: I was speaking metaphorically.

INTERVIEWER: But you wouldn't deny that America the Super has done a lot for Mr. Gold's campaign. Are some of the funders of your Super PAC expecting some quid pro quo?

SUPER PAC CEO: Done a lot! Was sitting up half the night with him when he had chicken pox a lot? Was schlepping him to band practice all those years a lot? Do I ask for thanks? No. A mother doesn't ask for thanks. You do for people, you do for people, and where does it get you? I'll tell you where it gets you: No communication. No coordination. By law, a Super PAC cannot coordinate or communicate with a candidate's campaign.

26.

←——→

August Surprise

Todd Akin's rather singular theology
Rejected what's in middle-school biology
And treated basic research with defiance.
His House committee dealt, of course, with science.
He ran for a Missouri Senate seat
Whose holder looked quite easy to defeat.
But then he said, with customary piety,
That rape, of the "legitimate" variety,
Will rarely make one pregnant, since the shock
Will put the reproductive works on lock.
(This proves at least he isn't thinking maybe
A kindly stork is what will bring a baby.)
Republicans, appalled, said "Todd, skiddoo!"
Though language in a bill that they'd pushed through
The House was close to his. Plus their right flank
Had in the party platform placed a plank

Against abortion, and the way they framed
The language, there were no exceptions named.
Paul Ryan was a sponsor of that bill—
Which meant that Akin's ignorance would spill
Into the presidential race for sure.
Republicans were braced now to endure
A charge they'd heard a million times before:
On women they were surely waging war.

The Female Reproductive System

*(A lecture by Representative Todd Akin, a member of the House
Committee on Science, Space, and Technology)*

Legitimate rape will just shut the thing down.
So if she gets pregnant, it shows that her gown
Was cut way too low or she had on a skirt
So tight it revealed an intention to flirt.
In some way she wanted to show off her shape.
And thus it was not a legitimate rape.

Legitimate rape will stop the thing cold.
So if she gets pregnant she might not have told
The fellow to stop, and not be so rough—
Or maybe she told him, but not loud enough.
Or utterly failed to make good her escape.
And thus it was not a legitimate rape.

27.

←——→

Reaching the Starting Line

As delegates prepared for their excursions
To Tampa, Romney faced some more diversions.
For one, a hurricane was on its way;
That forced the cancellation of one day.
The winds turned west, but speakers would perform
In TV competition with a storm.

The Show Must Go On

Republicans wonder how they will fare
With Anderson Cooper not even there.

The fervent followers of Dr. Paul
Then staged a small kerfuffle in the hall.
In Tampa, Mitt's men had to have a plan,
Some said, to somehow humanize their man.
But Mitt would share his innermost concerns
Around the time he showed his tax returns.
Reveal himself? No, Mitt would not be forced;
The humanizing had to be outsourced.
And so Ann Romney, Mitt's appealing bride,
Proclaimed there was a human being inside
This mannequin. Of this she seemed assured.
No details, though. We'd have to take her word.
The delegates went wild when Ryan fed
To them much meat that was the deepest red—
Though tainted by his facts, so checkers said.
They said he'd lied, or certainly misled.
Clint Eastwood's turn on stage was so bizarre
It was more memorable than Mitt's by far.
It seemed like Clint, his chair, and their vignette
Had wandered in from some adjoining set.
Mitt Romney asked us all to contemplate
If we are better off than in '08.
Though he neglected mentioning our troops.
(Did Perry, watching, silently say "Oops"?)
Mitt did speak well, but still did not illumine
The question on folks' minds: Is this dude human?

Calling In the Humanizer Man

Analysts say that Romney campaign strategists face the
challenge of humanizing their candidate.

— News reports

They'd like it if this man the folks are seeing
Resembled more an actual human being.
For that he'd need some warmth and schmaltz and soul;
Then he'd appear less cut-out and more whole.
So in their dreams of triumph they aspire
To show that their guy bleeds and may perspire.
This can be done at once, without delay:
The Humanizer Man is on his way.

Yes, any candidate with boardlike stiffness
Can be adjusted with surprising swiftness.
The Humanizer Man's done this before.
Though he fell short of loosening Al Gore,
He's had a host of triumphs in his day.
So if Mitt's men believe, to their dismay,
Their man's as human as a Charolais,
It isn't hard to make things A-OK.
They simply need to go to him and say,
"The Humanizer Man is on his way."

A few days later, pollsters would announce
The absence of a Mitt convention bounce.
The undecideds still would not decide;
Essentially, the candidates were tied
As Democrats prepared to cheer their cheers
In Charlotte in support of "Four More Years."
Festivities were bound to start off well:
The not-so-secret weapon was Michelle.
She was, in polls, the most adored Obama.
The role she seemed to revel in: First Mama.
About her speech encomia were written.
The Charlotte delegates were plainly smitten.
The platform's words, though, critics said, ignored
Jerusalem and mentioned not the Lord.
So missing passages were then restored,
With machinations some saw as untoward.
The bloggers might have made this all the rage,
Except that night Bill Clinton took the stage.
Addressing crowds, he somehow strikes a tone
That seems to be for you and you alone,
As if you two are walking arm in arm.
He spoke with clarity, he spoke with charm,
And what he asked that Charlotte night was whether
You're on your own or we're in this together.
Obama's speech was good, of course, whereas
Bill Clinton gave a speech with real pizzazz.
Upstaged? Well, yes, but by a speech with flair,
And not by Eastwood and an empty chair.

Convention Bounce

From Charlotte, Obama had hoped for a bounce.
It came in a way unforeseen:
When William J. Clinton had spoken his piece,
He'd furnished a strong trampoline.

28.

September Surprise

September's job report was disappointing.
That didn't mean that folks were now anointing
Mitt Romney as the President to be.
In fact, the pundits all agreed that he
Had lots of work to do to crack the code
That might yet make the White House his abode.
The polls on Medicare had now adjusted;
They showed the Democrats again more trusted,
And Medicare, the pollsters soon found out
Was something voters truly cared about.
On economic issues Mitt had led;
The polls now showed Obama was ahead.
Responding to some embassy attacks,
Mitt fumbled both his timing and the facts.
What made Mitt's odd response so consequential
Was this: It simply wasn't presidential.

It led Barack Obama to proclaim
Mitt liked to fire first and then take aim.
Some asked which campaign hand had made the slip
That let Mitt shoot this wild shot from the hip.
From his own party, critics had begun
To question how the Mitt campaign was run.
One thought few party loyalists disputed:
The Mitt campaign just had to be rebooted.

A Rallying Cry from the Romney Camp

Amid Discord, Romney Seeks to Sharpen Message on His Agenda

—*New York Times* headline

We've got to go now hell for leather.
We've got to get our act together,
'Cause even right-wing pundits say
That this campaign's in disarray.
We must confess it's such a mess
We find it difficult to press
Our message that this country needs
A man who's proven by his deeds
That he can turn a firm around,
That he is someone who's renowned
For skills in management writ large.
But wait: That's who we've got in charge.

The next misstep the party would bemoan
Was made by Mitt entirely on his own.
While on the coast of Florida in May,
Behind closed doors he'd managed to convey
A stark contempt, as if he were Ayn Rand,
For nearly half the people in the land.
They paid no income tax, he said, and should
Be written off as wed to victimhood.
He'd not engage, he said, in the futility
Of urging them to take responsibility
For their own lives, because they'd never do it.
It would be wasted effort to pursue it.
A camera was there, behind some fern.
(One wonders: Will these people never learn?)
The tape was aired. A firestorm began,
Diverting Mitt from his rebooting plan.
And even party loyalists were shaken:
Some thought they might as well have run Todd Akin.
The press said this was truly Mitt, denuded.
The group he'd cruelly written off included
Some people whose support he most desired—
Say, wounded vets and old folks who'd retired.
And some, with payroll tax they do submit,
Were paying at a higher rate than Mitt.

I've Got the Mitt Thinks I'm a Moocher, a Taker Not a Maker, Blues

(Sung by three members of the 47 percent)

Well, I work two jobs and that makes for a kinda long day.
And the boss deducts the payroll tax that I've gotta pay.
With sales tax, too, I kinda thought I was paying my dues.
I've got the Mitt thinks I'm a moocher, a taker not a maker,
    blues.

Well, the wife and I took retirement some years ago.
And social security accounts for most of our dough.
Though we contributed to that so we'd have it there to use.
I've got the Mitt thinks I'm a moocher, a taker not a maker,
    blues.

Well I went to 'Nam while Mitt went on his mission to
    France.
A buddy needed rescuin' and I thought, "Well, I'll take a
    chance."
A wounded-vet pension's not the salary that I would
    choose.
I've got the Mitt thinks I'm a moocher, a taker not a maker,
    blues.

(All, in chorus)
Yes, he thinks we're bums, and work is something we would
    refuse.

Entitlements, he says, are what we just live to abuse.
With his fat cat friends what he says about us is *j'accuse*.
So some of us moochers would sure like to see him lose.
We've got the Mitt thinks that we're moochers, takers and
     not makers, blues.

It was, some said, the worst campaign week ever—
And one that could torpedo Mitt's endeavor.
The problem that the swing-state polls defined:
The race was close, but Romney was behind;
While Romney's share of swing-state polls was sinking,
The "undecided" slice of polls was shrinking.
Some party chiefs were daunted by Mitt's lag.
They'd once thought that they had this in the bag.
Some right-wing commentators were aghast.
They said that something had to change—and fast.

29.

Falling Back

Amidst all this, Mitt Romney could at least
Refer to turmoil in the Middle East
As one example illustrating how
Stability and long-term peace is now
In that sad region further out of reach
Than when Obama gave his Cairo speech.
Mitt said we'd been too quick to spare the rod
In Syria, when dealing with Assad,
And hadn't made it clear how we will ban
The bomb from all those mad dogs in Iran.

Romney Outsources His Foreign Policy to the Neoconservatives

> *After 9/11, the neocons captured one Republican*
> *president who was naïve about the world. Now . . . they*
> *have captured another would-be Republican president*
> *and vice president, both jejune about the world.*
> —*Maureen Dowd,* The New York Times

Advisers to Mitt from the neocon right
Believe that America must show its might.
Though draft dodgers all, they're in favor of force—
With other folks' kids on the front lines, of course.
Through Romney's campaign, they have all slithered back—
The people who brought you the war in Iraq.

Obama's weak, Mitt tried hard to contend—
Although considering Osama's end,
That notion wasn't such an easy sell.
And some thought it would not help Mitt to dwell
On matters like what touched off Mideast mobs
Instead of concentrating hard on jobs.
He'd started out by saying that's what mattered,
But now the shots from Mitt's campaign seemed scattered.
Barack's convention bounce did not recede,

And gradually he opened up a lead.
Mitt's team was braced for what the polls were bringing:
That states that swung were now no longer swinging.
Yes, in Ohio, many polls would find
That Mitt was ten percentage points behind.

Ohio

(A reprise sung by Republicans)

Why, oh why, oh why-oh?
Why are we losing in Ohio?
Why is this our fate in our golden-ring state?
This simply doesn't compute.

What a lame campaigner!
Given his gaffes, Mitt should stay mute.
Oh why, oh why-oh, should we lose Ohio?
How could we ever have chosen this guy-oh?
Maybe we should have picked Newt.

When analysts then analyzed the polling,
Some said the bell for Mitt's campaign was tolling.
Some right-wing bloggers said that they would guess
That pollsters are as biased as the press.
The Romney campaign spokesmen said, "Just wait:

Our man will crush him in the first debate."
The pundits said, whenever they'd expound,
Mitt still had time to turn this thing around.
But, given early voting, they would note,
Some states had folks now lining up to vote.

30.

←———→

First Debate

From pols and pundits, therefore, what we heard
Was that the first debate, October third,
Was something close to Romney's do or die.
Advice to him was not in short supply.
Aggressiveness is good, said some, although
Not so aggressive that you fail to show
You're likable. (Well, sort of—more or less.)
Remember that when starting to aggress.
Specifics, some said, were what Romney needs—
Though those could get him lost among the weeds.
So no specifics? Or should Romney fling
Some zingers, or embrace the vision thing?
Newt Gingrich, who, to judge by his career,
Might counsel Mitt to bite Obama's ear,
Was much less snarky, offering advice
That humor often proves a great device—

Though laughs from Mitt would be an aberration
As likely as some aural mastication.

Newt Gingrich's Deepest Feelings About Mitt Romney's Upcoming Debate with Barack Obama

(Sung standing alone on center stage, illuminated by a single spot, during a guest appearance by the Speaker on Glee*)*

Our candidate must—and right here is the key—
Express big ideas, as big as the sea.
He must fill our base with tremendous esprit.
With supersized schemes, he must show just how he
Will see that free enterprise always stays free.
He must be heroic, like some Maccabee.
The bottom line, friends, is so simple to see.
It should have been me! Oh yes, don't you agree?
It should have been me! Yes, it. Should. Have. Been. Me!

In all, this first debate was heavy going.
Statistics fail to get the juices flowing.
It got so thick, so lacking in one-liners,
Some people fell asleep in their recliners.
Of those awake when all was said and done,
Most had this thought: The challenger had won.
Mitt's answers, whether factual or not,

Were clear and crisp, and all those answers got
Delivered with a quite commanding style.
The President seemed listless all the while—
Less certain of the points that he would share
And wishing he were anyplace but there.
So Democrats looked on with some dismay.
"The President," some said, "is MIA."
No traps were sprung; no knockout blows were struck.
But Mitt's campaign at last had got unstuck.
In spin-room chats, his men were all aglow.
Barack, they said, no longer had Big Mo.
The press found this a scrumptious dish to swallow.
It meant there was a horse race still to follow.
So in the dozen days folks had to wait
To watch once more those two men in debate
They tuned to cable, hearing pundits speak
On why Barack Obama'd been so weak,
And why the man had even failed to mention
The Mitt remarks that riled up such contention:
That video, sent Democrats from heaven,
In which Mitt says exactly forty-seven
Percent of us play victims, with the goal
Of living lives as moochers on the dole—
A speech for weeks Mitt would not disavow.
"Completely wrong" is what he called it now.

Mitt Doesn't Think That Nearly Half the People in This Country Are Moochers After All

After weeks of acknowledging only that his 47-percent remarks were "not elegantly stated," Mitt Romney now says that they were "just completely wrong."

—News reports

He was, he says, completely wrong;
To care for everyone is vital.
He's singing now a different song,
And "Etch A Sketch" is that song's title.

With Mitt called winner of the first debate
Republicans began to celebrate.
Another job report was then released.
That grim percentage had at last decreased,
Though not at an accelerated rate.
The figure now, at last, was under eight.
"Conspiracy!" the right-wing bloggers cried:
The numbers had been cooked, or maybe fried,
To serve some liberal reelection goals—
Exactly what they'd said about the polls.
But soon they had no reason to complain.
The President, reporting made it plain,
Had lost his lead. The latest polls had shown it.
In just one night, some said, Obama'd blown it.

31.

Obama Redux

A message by the voters had been sent:
They found Mitt credible as president.
And now some Democrats began to panic.
Was that debate, they asked, Barack's *Titanic*?
In this great orator, whom they'd revered,
Had every ounce of mojo disappeared?
And could, by chance, Republicans be right
That he'd become just too used up to fight?
The Democrats now found themselves conceding
Obama's standing in the polls was bleeding.
As Biden's night approached, they hoped that Joe
Could staunch that, or at least could slow the flow.
It's possible that Biden got that done.
Though pollsters disagreed on just who won,
The veep at least had focused some attention
On facts his boss had somehow failed to mention—

Like how Mitt's scorn for poorer people soars
When he and fat cats talk behind closed doors.
This veep debate became a little snarky,
With Biden calling Ryan claims malarkey.
They clashed on numbers and they clashed on facts.
They clashed on who should pay how much in tax.

A Simple Guide to Every Single Republican Tax Proposal Ever Made

(As verified by 178 independent studies)

Sure, sometimes they call it supply-side,
And sometimes they say job creation
Is risked if our entrepreneurs
Think profits get snatched by taxation.

It comes to the same simple credo
Around which the party has danced:
If rich people pay less in taxes,
Then everyone's life is enhanced.

Joe Biden from the start had come out slugging.
Though Ryan's team said what came out was mugging.
Joe's smile, Dems said, would not have been so visible
If things that Ryan said had been less risible.
This tussle was, no matter how it went,
Just warm-up for the next week's main event.

The Democrats, with fears he might lose twice,
Bombarded B. Obama with advice.
It turned out that they had no need to worry,
Obama took command, and in a hurry.
He didn't seem the same guy as before.
He won, said pollsters who were keeping score.
Though neither toward the other was benign,
Mitt seemed at times the one who crossed the line:
Toward both the moderator and his foe
He acted like a bossy CEO.
And also, said the tweets and posts and e-mails,
With his remarks he'd lost some ground with females.
He said he'd asked (not true, as it transpired)
For names of able women to be hired
When he became the boss in Boston, Mass.—
To crack the ceiling that they faced of glass.
Thus "binders full of women" was a phrase
That banged around the Internet for days.
The ref was Candy Crowley for this brawl,
The head butts and the gouges hers to call.
Benghazi's muddled tale, Mitt had a hunch,
Was where he'd likely land a roundhouse punch.
It seemed to be a weakness to exploit,
But Mitt at trying that proved maladroit.

Romney Attacks Obama on His First Response to the Benghazi Killings
(Or, We Never Promised You a Rose Garden)

Mitt thought O's response had not talked about terror.
Of that he was certain, but he was in error.
A warning was sent, but one Mitt failed to heed:
Obama, politely, had said "Please, proceed."
'Twas Crowley who told Mitt, and left him dejected—
A pushy A-student by teacher corrected.
He'd laid out a trap, and then *Snap!* The next minute
The Mittster himself was the one who'd stepped in it.

The Fox News types said everyone's aware
That Candy Crowley was, of course, unfair.
In their religion one can seem quite pious
By blaming everything on liberal bias.

32.

The Stretch

Within a day, the pollsters would announce
Obama's win did not give him a bounce.
So, at a rate that liberals found quite frightening,
The margins in the swing states kept on tightening.
The message that the pollsters now were sending:
Obama led, but Romney was ascending.
At last Mitt had the traction he had sought.
His guys were energized, and they all thought
That in the foreign policy debate
Mitt Romney's job was just to demonstrate
He was a calm and level-headed guy
Who valued peace, and wasn't going to try
To solve our foreign issues with more war—
No matter what he'd said a month before.
So, quickly, with astonishing velocity,
He scrubbed away all signs of bellicosity.

The policies he'd hastened to malign
As weak and ineffective were now fine.

Romney Beats His Swords into Plowshares

Mitt seemed to agree with Obama a lot.
Divergence in policy got hard to spot.
He used all the moderate words he could muster.
So where was the Mittster's past neocon bluster?
He knew that those still undecided would hate it.
The answer then is that the Etch A Sketch ate it.

Though he had lost, the Mittster didn't trip
In managing to execute this flip.
He'd done, some theorized, what needed doing:
Assured the folks that he'd not be pursuing
Some aims that could bring war without cessation —
The aims he'd backed to get the nomination.
And so, with only two short weeks to go,
Mitt had, he claimed incessantly, Big Mo.
Reporters went along, though some then noted
That states where some folks had already voted
And battlegrounds that Mitt would surely need
Still showed Obama with a narrow lead.
Mitt did make progress with the gender gap —
But then some ally'd open up his yap

And show, as middle-road as Mitt might seem,
The views of those who backed him were extreme.

Three Republican Candidates Discourse on the Subject of Rape
(And a fourth remains exceedingly quiet)

Legitimate rape, so we're told by Todd Akin,
Will not produce children but simply awaken
Defensive biology. That quickly locks
The system all down, just as safe as Fort Knox.

Joe Walsh says exceptions for "life of the mother"
Are phony exceptions, just like all the other
Exceptions suggested. Walsh says it's all jive,
Since doctors can always keep momma alive.

Now Mourdock says rapists' seed must be defended.
A pity, he says, but it's what God intended.
This absolute stance to which Mourdock still cleaves
Just happens to be what Paul Ryan believes.

The Rape Science Three can provide more reminders
That now Mitt's got wingnuts in all of those binders.

Whatever Mitt might confidently say,
That narrow lead had still not gone away.
But Mitt's men said what polls did not reveal
Was what their people had, and that was zeal.

33.

←————→

The Stretch of the Stretch

Ten days from being pictured in the booth,
Barack and Mitt were at it nail and tooth—
So many ads in swing states, crude or clever,
That voters started saying, "Sure. Whatever."
Mitt's strategy had not remained a riddle:
The newest Mitt was easing toward the middle.
With independent voters always wary
Of candidates who seem the least bit scary,
Mitt turned the right-wing volume down, which led
To his forgetting many things he'd said
While, running for the nomination, he
Had tried to suit his Party to a Tea.
Conservative? Well, sort of, but not nearly
What some (say, Mitt himself) had called severely.

Mitt Romney Beats His Plowshares into Feather Dusters

In Dwindling Days of the Race, Romney Takes a Softer Tack

—New York Times headline

Though disagree we might, I hold the view
That Democrats do love this country, too.
The leaders of both parties ought to chat.
In my home state, we did exactly that.
I've got a new respect for single mothers.
Their burden is much heavier than others'.
And, short of backing marriage, there are ways
That we can be both fair and kind to gays.
And when a great disaster takes its toll,
Then, certainly, the feds have got a role.
In fact, in office I would not evade
The chance to come to any victim's aid.
Need proof that these beliefs are at my core?
Just check my Senate race in '94—
'Cause then, like now, these views were apropos,
And that was only seven Mitts ago.

With fears of Sandy and its water rising,
Mitt's FEMA views required some revising.

Democracy
(A patriotic hymn for Republicans)

> *Despite the fact that incidents of in-person voter fraud in*
> *the United States are exceedingly rare, the GOP has used*
> *the issue to tighten election laws around the country.*
>   —*News reports*

American children are all taught in school
That voting's democracy's most vital tool.
But in the wrong hands all that voting can bring
A little too much of a very good thing.
Yes, too many voters of darker complexion
Can cause the wrong person to win an election.
And college kids mostly are just in a phase
That makes them left-wing and supportive of gays.
To us, each of them is a dangerous blighter
Whose voting should wait 'til he's older and whiter.
So we put in laws we have reason to think
Will mean that the strength of these voters will shrink.
We shorten the hours, and ask for a lot
Of picture IDs—more than anyone's got.
Their votes aren't the votes that the Framers intended.
We only regret that the Poll Tax has ended.
The voting we need in this land of the free
Is voting by people with whom we agree.

He tried—and this was not at all surprising—
To walk back all that talk of privatizing.
When Sandy called a halt to his campaign,
He plainly lacked a way to share folks' pain.
Barack Obama now was taking charge;
In times like these, a president looms large.
So Mitt just watched, as in these closing days
Both FEMA and Barack got heaped with praise.
And who had praised the president the most?
Chris Christie, former foe, now Jersey host.
The man who'd been like Romney's alter ego
Now cheered Obama as his best amigo.
The pair of them, one slim and one quite lardy,
Looked from afar a bit like Laurel and Hardy—
Although as Christie's paeans grew more numerous,
Their act struck Romney's team as far from humorous.
The storm was mentioned, too, when Bloomberg wrote,
In Bloomberg News, Obama had his vote.
So, though Mitt's houses were on high, dry land, he
Had come out with some damages from Sandy.
Both candidates gave closing talks, as planned,
And then the time for voting was at hand.
So now the two campaigns had matching goals:
Make sure their people made it to the polls.
Since who could vote would surely be disputed,
Vast throngs of party lawyers were recruited.

When, finally, the voting did begin,
Obama's lead seemed firm but razor thin.
Some pundits guessed, as lines and lawsuits mounted,
It might be days before all votes got counted.
But such predictions turned out to be wrong.
The wait for the results did not last long.
In maps that network anchors kept in view,
The swing states, one by one, got colored blue.
As Romney's routes to victory diminished,
The die was cast. This long campaign was finished—
A fact that some found hard to comprehend,
Since they'd been thinking it would never end.
The polls no longer occupied our time.
With speeches gone, the silence was sublime.
Auteurs of cutting ads had sheathed their knives.
Ohio folks could get back to their lives.
They answer telephones without the fear
That questions from a pollster's what they'll hear,
And pop off to the grocery if they choose,
Without the fear of being on the news.

Ohio Ends a Swing-State Phase

Of course it's an honor to be called by all,
The state that elects the commander in chief.
But now that it's over the sound around here
Is not lots of weeping but sighs of relief.

But in just thirty months it starts again.
Before that time the handlers will unpen
New candidates who they think have the grit
To do ferocious battle in the pit.
And pampered billionaires whose charm consists
Of wads of dirty money in their fists
Will on the sidelines scrutinize the pack,
Deciding which competitor to back.
About to battle for the laurel wreath,
The candidates will growl, and bare their teeth.
Dogfight!

ABOUT THE AUTHOR

A longtime staff writer at *The New Yorker,* Calvin Trillin is also *The Nation's* deadline poet, at a fee he has been complaining about since 1990. His acclaimed books range from the memoir *About Alice* to *Quite Enough of Calvin Trillin: Forty Years of Funny Stuff.* He lives in New York.

The text of this book is set in a sans serif face called Meta. One of the new modern faces of the past twenty years, it was designed by Erik Spiekermann. Meta was originally conceived for the German subway system, but has quickly become one of the most popular typefaces and is often seen in magazines and books.